Sammy Franco

KILLER INSTINCT

Unarmed Combat for Street Survival

Also by Sammy Franco

Survival Weapons
Sucker Punch
Cane Fighting
Double End Bag Training
The Heavy Bag Bible
The Widow Maker Compendium
Invincible: Mental Toughness Techniques for Peak Performance
Unleash Hell: A Step-by-Step Guide to Devastating Widow Maker Combinations
Feral Fighting: Advanced Widow Maker Fighting Techniques
The Widow Maker Program: Extreme Self-Defense for Deadly Force Situations
Savage Street Fighting: Tactical Savagery as a Last Resort
Heavy Bag Workout
Heavy Bag Combinations
Heavy Bag Training
The Complete Body Opponent Bag Book
Stand and Deliver: A Street Warrior's Guide to Tactical Combat Stances
Maximum Damage: Hidden Secrets Behind Brutal Fighting Combinations
First Strike: End a Fight in Ten Seconds or Less!
The Bigger They Are, The Harder They Fall
Self-Defense Tips and Tricks
Kubotan Power: Quick & Simple Steps to Mastering the Kubotan Keychain
Gun Safety: For Home Defense and Concealed Carry
Out of the Cage: A Guide to Beating a Mixed Martial Artist on the Street
Warrior Wisdom: Inspiring Ideas from the World's Greatest Warriors
War Machine: How to Transform Yourself Into a Vicious and Deadly Street Fighter
1001 Street Fighting Secrets
When Seconds Count: Self-Defense for the Real World
Street Lethal: Unarmed Urban Combat

Killer Instinct: Unarmed Combat for Street Survival
Copyright © 1991, 2017 by Sammy Franco
ISBN: 978-1-941845-45-5
Printed in the United States of America

Published by Contemporary Fighting Arts, LLC.
Visit us Online at: **SammyFranco.com**

For author interviews or publicity information, please send inquiries in care

"We accept the verdict of the past until the need for change cries out loudly enough to force upon us a choice between the comfort of further inertia and the irksomeness of action."

–*Learned Hand*

This book is for Carl Sosebee, who holds my friendship, respect, and admiration.

Contents

Warning!

The self-defense techniques, tactics, methods, and information described and depicted in this book can be dangerous and could result in serious injury and or death and should not be used or practiced in any way without the guidance of a professional reality based self-defense instructor.

The author, publisher, and distributors of this book disclaim any liability from loss, injury, or damage, personal or otherwise, resulting from the information and procedures in this book. *This book is for academic study only.*

Before you begin any exercise program, including those suggested in this book, it is important to check with your physician to see if you have any condition that might be aggravated by strenuous exercise.

VIII

Preface

Since publication of **Street Lethal: Unarmed Urban Combat,**
I have received hundreds of inquiries on Contemporary Fighting
Arts. Many relate to basic physical aspects of the system, such as
tools, techniques, footwork, equipment, training, and conditioning.
This is not surprising given the book's emphasis on the basic physical
components of the system. I was surprised, however, by the number
of people expressing their views on spiritual topics, and the even
greater number of responses concerning psychological, strategic, and
philosophical aspects of Contemporary Fighting Arts.

This book is in response to those interested in the mental
components of my art. It does not include every strategic and
psychological principle of the system. Nonetheless, I have attempted
to provide a thorough and provocative look at Contemporary
Fighting Arts.

I believe this book will enhance your fighting skills regardless
of your rank or particular style. However, beginners are encouraged
to read Street Lethal to gain a better understanding of the stance,
offensive and defensive tools, and other introductory principles of the
art. Advanced practitioners can launch straight ahead with this text.
For the convenience of all readers, I have included a glossary of more
than two hundred terms.

Finally, this book is not a compilation of theories. The concepts
and principles of Contemporary Fighting Arts, although developed
and refined in the laboratory, have been tested and proven in
reality. I am confident that my system embodies scientifically sound
methodologies of unarmed fighting. After all, unarmed combat is as
much a science as an art. Contemporary Fighting Arts will withstand

skepticism and challenge.

I urge you to use this knowledge in the true spirit of the martial way. May your path be peaceful and unmarred by violence.

- Sammy Franco
SammyFranco.com

Introduction

KILLER INSTINCT

Evolution in the Martial Arts

The history of the ancient fighting arts is a vast subject. Volumes have been written, and still the topic is clouded by uncertainty. Man has been warring longer than he has been recording events. Perhaps in some ancient cave, an early warrior first contemplated the best and safest way to crack his enemy's skull. If so, he was the first martial artist, albeit a very primitive one.

It is impossible to say when man first began to look upon warfare as an art and a science. The earliest techniques of unarmed combat were probably passed in secrecy from teacher to student before any particular method of fighting was formalized into an identifiable system. Some historians believe Chinese boxing may have begun around 206 b.c. to 220 a.d. One very popular theory is that Asian fighting arts were cultivated around the teachings of the Buddhist patriarch Bodhidharma in the sixth century. Bodhidharma is known as Tamo by the Chinese, Daruma Daishi by the Japanese.

Bodhidharma traveled from India to China spreading the earliest tenets of Buddhism. His journey led him to the Honan province of China. The enlightened monks of the Shaolin Monastery were the beneficiaries of Bodhidharma's teachings. Various meditations, as well as physical, mental, and spiritual exercises, were incorporated into their religious programs. In time, the monks refined and developed particular movements and philosophies into what later became Chinese boxing, "Ch'uan-fa," or "Ch'uan-shu." To this day, many consider the Shaolin Temple to be the birthplace of the Asian martial arts.

Chinese martial techniques spread to Japan, Okinawa, Korea, and other parts of Southeast Asia, where they were incorporated into existing methods and ultimately developed into various unique styles of combat. This evolutionary process led to hundreds of different styles and systems. The differences in the various styles are attributable to a variety of factors and influences. Geography, culture, religion, and means of warfare all dramatically influenced the development and modification of combat systems.

Historians attribute the development of high-line kicks in the northern Chinese styles to the tall, grassy plains where combat was waged. In contrast, the quick, tight-hand techniques and lower stance of some southern Chinese styles are linked to crowded urban environments. Some analysts believe geographical proximity between northern China and Korea and southern China and Okinawa explain the spectacular kicking techniques of Korean karate and the powerful hand techniques of Okinawan karate. Today, Chinese kung-fu practitioners continue to wear soft cotton shoes, while certain karateka practice barefoot. This is a carry-over from the various terrains where the styles originated. Kung-fu grew in a rocky, unstable land. Barefoot styles, such as Okinawan karate, originated in sandy, relatively soft terrain. Take a look at the flashy jump kicks employed in many styles. This type of kick is linked to a particular means of warfare. It was used to knock charging aggressors from their horses.

Other methods of warfare greatly influenced unarmed combat techniques. Use of the sword, stick, and dagger affected the body mechanics of empty-hand techniques. Consider, for example, the traditional method of launching punches from the hip. The hip punch generates tremendous force as a result of the physical laws called into play. The punch, however, exposes the centerline and upper gates to attack and loses some of its effectiveness to telegraphing. It is likely that the hip punch is an unarmed relative of movements and techniques originating with swords and daggers.

Unarmed Combat for Street Survival

Religion and philosophy have also played significant roles in the development of traditional martial techniques. The peaceful and holistic views of Buddhism, Taoism, and Shintoism have produced venerable masters whose arts are predicated on peace and harmony. Aikido is a good example of a style designed to preserve and protect life. Aikido uses very sophisticated throws, holds, and joint locks whenever possible, rather than destructive blows and kicks. In addition, certain animistic belief systems have led to styles modeled on the nature and spirit of animals. Consider the five animal forms of kung-fu: dragon, tiger, leopard, crane, and snake. Other styles include the monkey, eagle claw, and mantis.

Early waves of Asian immigration brought the martial arts to the United States. However, cultural differences and discrimination resulted in segregation, and the Eastern fighting arts were not openly practiced or shared. Consequently, for a significant period of time, Americans did not benefit from the cultural richness of the East. It was not until after World War II and the Korean War that Americans were initiated into various sublime arts of the East. Returning servicemen and new immigrants brought such arts as judo and taekwon-do to the States. Yet, martial arts did not really begin to proliferate in America until the 1960s, when television, Hollywood, and superstars like Bruce Lee opened America's eyes to the impressive possibilities of the Asian fighting arts.

A great deal of change has taken place in the arts over the last thirty years. Various traditional schools and styles have been modified and refined. Radical changes have taken place with the modernist trend. Some of these changes have been positive, and some have been very negative. In addition to changes in the world of martial arts, America itself has undergone radical transformations. Unfortunately, much of the good is overshadowed by the bad. Many people believe America is in the grips of a social, cultural, and spiritual crisis.

Modern-day America is plagued by a national epidemic of violent crime. Drug wars, brutal homicides, assaults, and rapes are tragic realities of everyday life. I am convinced that violence and aggression are cultivated and condoned in American culture. I certainly am not alone in this assessment. Among my colleagues are professionals whose jobs have carried them to various countries. Their qualified discussions with many different foreign nationals support the notion that America is viewed as the most pathological and randomly violent society on the planet. It may sound cynical, but this mind-set is evident in our art and entertainment. Take a look at America's favorite sport, football. It epitomizes the aggressiveness of our culture. Watch a game and you'll observe some interesting things, like the tremendous power and strength of a 280-pound lineman moving with the speed of a panther in an all-out effort to crush the quarterback. Pain is exulted; I've heard of a player who continued in a game after having torn off his fingertip.

Football epitomizes the aggression and violence that is so ingrained in American culture.

Unarmed Combat for Street Survival

I'm also amazed by boxing and hockey. It's incredible to see how hostile and aggressive the crowd becomes. Is it the roar of an overly enthusiastic crowd, or are the fans screaming for the athletes to smash and injure each other in a vicious game of win or lose? I think many people unfortunately fall into the latter category, just as some are lured to car races by the possibility of a gruesome wreck.

Without a doubt, size, strength, and aggression are admired and condoned. Recent evidence indicates that a significant number of young American males are frequent users of anabolic steroids. These chemicals increase aggression, muscle mass, body weight, and endurance. It's that popular refrain, "Bigger is Better!" On top of all this, add the effects of PCP, ice, crack, and cocaine, and you've got a deadly brew, in more ways than one.

On the streets of America there is no bushido, the honorable code of the ancient warrior. Today's serious martial artist must be prepared to neutralize steroid-induced mesomorphs or raving lunatics high on deadly drugs. Much of what we have learned and been prepared for in

It's ugly but true, American fans love a good bloody fight. Here, two hockey player slug it out, giving the fans their moneys worth.

the safety of the dojo will not work on the streets. A good streetfighter can be a vicious animal unrestricted by rules of combat etiquette. Many traditional approaches and techniques will not work.

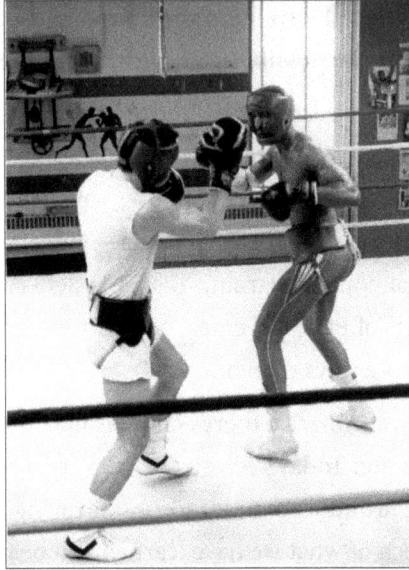

The traditional sparring practice of western boxing is in adequate training for the aggressiveness and potential horror of a street fight.

And success and failure can mean the difference between life and death. It is not my intention to disparage the traditional arts and the many great masters of yesterday and today. But, in all honesty, many things are being taught in the name of traditionalism that simply will not work outside the context of controlled sparring. In this regard, we can quickly survey some of the most obvious deficiencies of traditional approaches.

First, far too many traditional styles emphasize complex ornamental techniques. Good examples are the high-line kicks, which are great for demonstrations of balance, flexibility, and coordination, but too unreliable and inefficient for the street. Frankly, in terms of real fighting, you'd gain as much benefit from taking a good modern dance or ballet class as you would from spending a great deal of time perfecting high-line kicks. Never use a high-line kick in a streetfight. If you do, you are likely to end up on the ground before you know it, and from there you could end up in the hospital or morgue.

In today's society, the martial artist is likely to be confronted by extraordinarily powerful opponents. Consequently, Contemporary Fighting Arts promotes only the most efficient and effective fighting techniques.

Many traditionalists teach punching techniques that lack knock-down power and undermine defensive structures. A few examples are the backfist, jab, spinning backfists, and hip-launched punches. The backfist takes too long to execute if thrown with any power at all, and unless contact is just right, you can smash the intricate bones in the back of the hand. The jab, one of the most frequently thrown tools in kickboxing, is a probing punch designed to create openings for more devastating blows. However, a "feeler" is too risky in a real fight. It lacks power and prolongs the encounter, allowing an opponent the opportunity to gain the initiative and counter with viciousness. Spinning punches are out of the question. Granted, you can generate a lot of power by cranking the whole body behind such a punch, but you telegraph tremendously and run the risk of slipping and falling down. Finally, I am totally bewildered why so many teachers continue to promote the hip punch. It is too telegraphic, opens the centerline, and can be picked off by the most basic blocks.

Traditional stances vary greatly. The photo above demonstrates just about every conceivable strategic weakness.

Then there are the stances. There are more stances than exotic birds in the aviary of the national zoo. There are stances, believe it or not, that start virtually on the ground, stances based on one foot, stances with the hands held at the side, stances that completely open the upper and lower gates, and stances that allow you to get the jump on the opponent because he's laughing so hard. Regardless of these, the stance is the offensive and defensive foundation of a fighting system, and it must be strategically designed to afford maximum protection to your vital targets while allowing maximum capability for launching your offensive attack. Far too many traditionalists adhere to a particular stance, notwithstanding its weaknesses, simply because that's the way it has always been.

Another traditional fighting stance. Note the balance, foot placement, shoulder and body alignment, and hand positioning.

Another critical flaw in many styles is the lack of proficiency in all three ranges of combat. You will find specialization in only one range of encounter, at most two, even though range proficiency is essential to streetfighting. Some karateka excel in kicking range but lack strong punching skills. Grappling range is often totally overlooked. On the other hand, other arts such as judo concentrate entirely on grappling range and neglect punching and kicking ranges.

Current training methodologies are often unrealistic and impractical. Kata forms are a good example. Certainly, beneficial qualities are developed by the practice of kata. They enhance form, balance, coordination, speed, rhythm, and overall body awareness and control. On the psychological and spiritual levels, they provide an excellent vehicle for self-expression. It takes years of commitment and discipline to perfect forms. But forms are an end unto themselves. The grace and beauty of a flawless kata demonstration is a wonderful thing, but I've seen demonstrations by practitioners who would be demolished in short order by a vicious streetfighter. Forms have very little to do with real get-down-and-rumble fighting. Furthermore, the skills developed through the practice of kata may be gained in more realistic training such as shadowfighting.

In addition to training methodologies, much training equipment used today is actually outmoded. The makiwara board found in many dojos is not a great training device. A makiwara is a wooden striking post that is padded with straw and usually embedded in the ground or hung against the wall. It is struck repeatedly to develop power, calluses, and mental toughness, but it is not practical. First of all, it's a stationary target, unlike a heavy bag, double-end bag, or focus mitts, and oftentimes it is situated so that it restricts certain angles of attack. Furthermore, the makiwara is only one example of antiquated training equipment that can permanently damage or disfigure the hands and feet.

I believe tools, stances, techniques, footwork, strategies, and training methodologies must be challenged and ultimately changed to conform to reality. If you are going to survive on the streets against the meanest, theoretical principles must be sound and pragmatic to reduce vulnerabilities and achieve results. You'll need the skills and mentality to confront and cope with the horror of a vicious street encounter. This vision led to the creation and development of Contemporary Fighting Arts.

Author Sammy Franco demonstrates the fighting stance of Contemporary Fighting Arts. Note balance, foot positioning, hand arrangement, shoulder and body alignment, and head posture.

KILLER INSTINCT

Introduction
Exploring Contemporary Fighting Arts

KILLER INSTINCT

Contemporary Fighting Arts is a brutal martial art specifically designed for hard-core streetfighting. Unlike karate, kung-fu, or kickboxing, it is geared to the violence of American society. It is the product of years of research, experimentation, and modification. The physical characteristics of the art are based principally on the concept of stylistic integration.

Stylistic integration is a design strategy that identifies and incorporates the most efficient and effective tools and techniques for any combat scenario. Design integration is used in a variety of disciplines and pursuits other than the martial sciences. For example, race car engineers selectively amalgamate materials and components to achieve maximum speed, maneuverability, and endurance for particular races and courses. Weapon manufacturers work continuously to refine the hardware of war. In my case, I have employed the principles of stylistic integration to produce a system of unarmed combat that offers the fighter a brutal and efficient arsenal. But a weapon is only as good as the soldier trained to use it. The particular tools and techniques of Contemporary Fighting Arts are highly dependent upon the dedication, mentality, and strategic skills of the practitioner.

There are two very distinct schools of thought on stylistic integration and modification in the martial arts, commonly referred to as the "traditionalist" and "modernist" schools. Conservative traditionalists are ardently skeptical of any style or technique that has not existed for a very long time—centuries in some cases. Traditionalists proclaim that change is heresy and flat out reject any analysis or experimentation that they feel may water down or detract from the authenticity of a particular style. The danger of this rigid perspective should be obvious. It was this type of thinking that fostered belief in the Ptolemian model depicting the Earth as the center of all heavenly bodies. This erroneous belief continued in spite of the Copernican model, which correctly explained the relationship of planets, sun, and stars. Copernicus' model circulated underground for nearly a century because of ignorance. If you don't think this analogy applies to some die-hard traditionalists, think again. I know karateka who've been defeated on the street, but do you think they wised up and took a second look at their style or system? No way. They continue to believe that their system is the only system, their way is the only way, win or lose. Blind belief and adherence to unproven principles can be very dangerous.

The rigidity of the views of some traditionalists is ironic, since modification and evolution form the foundation of many well-established traditional systems. For example, judo is the evolutionary product of jigoro kano, aikido is the synthesis and refinement by Morihei Ueshiba of many styles and disciplines, and Kokaku Takeda developed daito ryu after a great deal of research and exploration.

On the opposite end of the spectrum from the traditionalists are the modernists. American modernism was ushered in by the late Bruce Lee. Few could dispute his contributions or his commitment to the arts. However, Mr. Lee's philosophical belief that a particular style or system restricted the "truth" and "life" of the martial way has been carried to a dangerous extreme by some thinkers who extol the wisdom and virtue of the "style of no style." These theorists promote "formlessness" in fighting. This excessive abstraction might be fun from an intellectual perspective but not much fun when it leaves you without a specific framework within which to advance or, more importantly, leaves you unprepared and without a solution to a very real and dangerous problem. I refer to this school of thought as the "unstructured modernists."

My approach is somewhere between these two extremes. Blind adherence to archaic patterns is not a viable alternative; yet, to abandon structure is to abandon the fundamentals of fighting.

Conceptualization shapes and molds combative characteristics, but it becomes useless if it is not solidly and safely actualized. Concrete systems, strategies, and methods produce efficiency and overall combative direction.

Contemporary Fighting Arts has extracted the safest and most effective tools from a variety of styles. These weapons are then modified, refined, and strategically arrayed around the ranges of unarmed combat, fighting environments, and other factors. Through proper and consistent training, these tools and techniques are maximized by the martial artist who attains self-knowledge, psychological preparedness, and mastery of the killer instinct.

To provide a better understanding of Contemporary Fighting Arts, I will present an overview of the system's three broad, but vital, components: the physical, the mental, and the spiritual.

The Physical Component

The physical component of Contemporary Fighting Arts focuses on the physical development of a martial artist. This includes combative fitness, tool development, and combative attributes.

Combative Fitness

You will not prevail in the streets unless you are well above average in physical fitness. Sure, there are some pretty mean barroom brawlers out there who spend more time lifting beer bottles than weights, but their victories more often than not result from animal attitudes and confrontations with unskilled opponents. Those tattooed, beer-swilling Camel smokers can be taken out every time by a physically fit and skilled martial artist. A word of caution, however: in addition to those untrained toughs, there are a lot of guys who have followed the American trend of spending more and more time on weight training and who are dying to demonstrate their physical prowess. The serious martial artist must be competitively conditioned to prevail against powerful opponents. Conditioning is vitally important. In fact, you cannot truly master combative tools and skills unless you're in excellent shape.

Skipping rope can be a very demanding exercise that requires a good amount of coordination.

Unfortunately, many teachers overlook the importance of physical conditioning. They accept monthly dues and leave it to the students to set the level and method of physical conditioning. Take the time to visit some dojos in your area. You'll be surprised by the waistlines and other indicators that many are doing little or nothing to achieve serious fitness. On the average, you'll have to spend more than one hour a day to achieve maximum fitness. Most people have such busy schedules that they can't make it to class every day. However, modern scientific and practical training methods will diminish the time you need to achieve optimum fighting shape.

In Contemporary Fighting Arts, combative fitness is comprised of two broad components: cardiorespiratory conditioning and muscular/skeletal conditioning. The cardiorespiratory system includes the heart, lungs, and circulatory system, which undergoes rapid and tremendous stress during unarmed combat. This system must supply the brain and muscles with freshly oxygenated blood to avoid instant fatigue.

Aerobic exercise is the best way to strengthen the cardiorespiratory system. To qualify as aerobic, an exercise must elevate the heart rate to a training level for a prolonged period, usually twenty to thirty minutes. Aerobic exercises should be performed at least four times per week. Excellent aerobic exercises include running, rope skipping, cycling, and swimming. Aerobic training must be performed consistently for maximum effectiveness.

Muscular/ skeletal conditioning refers to strength, endurance, and flexibility. Muscular strength is the force exerted by a particular muscle or muscle group against resistance. Muscular endurance is the ability of a particular muscle or muscle group to perform the same motion or task or hold a fixed contraction over time. Flexibility refers to the overall tone and the extension and retraction capabilities of the muscular/skeletal construction.

Muscular strength and endurance are developed by systematic and progressive overloads on the muscles. Although weight training is a very controversial subject in the martial arts, I believe it is the best way to develop muscular strength and endurance. I strongly disagree with those who maintain that weight lifting makes a fighter "muscle bound." To the contrary, a scientific weight training program combined with consistent stretching exercises will significantly improve power, endurance, speed, coordination, and even pain tolerance.

Contemporary Fighting Arts incorporates weight training for strength, muscle mass, and power.

Flexibility is important because it ensures muscle suppleness and the ability to move through the maximum natural ranges. While high-line kicks are not employed in Contemporary Fighting Arts, flexibility is still vital because it reduces the possibility of injury, promotes circulation, and diminishes tension. Stretching is something that should be performed before and after weight training and every other form of physical exertion. Every major muscle of the upper and lower body should be stretched progressively, with maximum stretch held for at least sixty seconds. Avoid ballistic stretching (i.e., bouncing or pulsing), which can tear and injure muscles, tendons, and ligaments. If you have time, yoga is an excellent method of achieving flexibility, not to mention tremendous mental calm and relaxation.

Stretching ensures muscle suppleness, promote circulation, and reduces tension.

An effective program for the cardiorespiratory and muscular/ skeletal systems will ensure proper body composition. Body composition is the ratio of fat tissue to lean tissue. Fat is fat, and lean tissue includes muscle, organs, cartilage, and other connective tissue. Ideal body fat composition is 6 to 10 percent for men and 8 to 10 percent for women. Trained technicians can measure body fat by a variety of methods, the two most popular being water submersion and skin-fold calipers.

Body composition will be significantly affected by diet as well as a particular training regimen. I believe in high carbohydrate intakes, as much as 70 percent of the fighter's daily caloric intake. Carbohydrates are the body's primary source of energy and are found in vegetables, fruits, potatoes, pasta, and all grain products.

In addition to carbohydrates, proteins are essential for muscle and tissue growth and repair. Poultry, fish, and legumes are excellent sources of low-fat proteins. Unless you are on a serious weight-gain program, which may require a more significant protein intake, I believe you can devote no more than 20 percent of your daily caloric intake to proteins.

Finally, unsaturated fats are vital to good health and should constitute approximately 10 percent of your calories. Don't confuse unsaturated fats with their nasty relatives, saturated fats. Saturated fats, found in ice cream, chocolate, cakes, and so on, are a big "no." Forget them, they will only make you fat and sluggish. Look for natural unsaturated fats in such foods as nuts, seeds, and various grains.

A final word on dieting. Athletes and trainers have come a long, long way in this area. Remember the days when a prize fighter would eat scrambled eggs, steak, and fried potatoes for breakfast? No more. Today's serious seeker of fitness has a great body of knowledge and expertise with which to consult in structuring the perfect dietary regimen for his or her purposes. There are a lot of fads, however, and you must be very careful about what you accept as truth. Play it safe and consult a nutritionist specializing in the care of athletes. Don't neglect this important aspect of combative fitness.

Tool Development

The physical component of Contemporary Fighting Arts requires mastery of the tools and techniques of the system. This includes the stance, offensive and defensive weapons, footwork, and various attributes of unarmed combat. Contemporary Fighting Arts is a striking art because striking is safer, more efficient, and unquestionably more definitive. We work our striking tools to bone-shattering levels.

Although punching-range tools are emphasized, kicking and grappling ranges cannot be neglected. Kicking-range tools consist of powerful and deceptive low-line kicks. Grappling-range tools exclude locks, chokes, and throws. Instead, we focus on head butts, elbows, knees, foot stomps, tearing, gouging, and even biting, if all else fails.

Although Contemporary Fighting Arts is predicated on the strong, offensive philosophy of "strike first with viciousness and ferocity," defensive skills are also important. A good defense is efficient, uncomplicated, and impenetrable. Our defensive structure provides the martial artist with maximum protection while allowing total freedom of choice for gaining offensive control. Our blocks, parries, and evasions are direct and to the point. Simplicity is the key.

Combat Attributes

Tools and techniques mean nothing unless combined and utilized properly. A kick, punch, or strike is useless unless employed with speed, power, timing, rhythm, coordination, accuracy, balance, and range specificity. These attributes apply to each particular offensive and defensive tool and technique. Each part must be brought together to form a unified whole. For example, a powerful punch is a great thing, and you can develop one through constant heavy-bag training. But unless you can pull it out and use it in the rapidly changing conditions of a real fight, what good is it? It's like an oversized racing piston lying on the mechanic's bench. It's a vital race component, but it must be incorporated into the harmonious structure of the whole engine before it serves its true purpose. Contemporary Fighting

Arts has three unique training methodologies to refine and enhance fundamental tools and attributes: proficiency, conditioning, and street training.

Proficiency training develops speed, power, accuracy, coordination, and balance. The martial artist sharpens one tool at a time by throwing it over and over again, for two- to three-hundred repetitions. Each is executed with perfect form and at various speeds. The tool is even practiced in the dark or with the eyes closed to develop a kinesthetic feel for the weapon. Proficiency training can be accomplished through the use of various types of equipment, including the heavy bag, double-end bag, focus mitts, kicking pads, foam shield, and a mirror.

The focus mitts are unsurpassed training tools in the hands of a skilled handler. Here, they are used for proficiency training.

Conditioning training develops endurance, rhythm, distancing, timing, speed, agility, footwork, and coordination. This type of training requires the martial artist to deliver a variety of offensive and defensive combinations for four-minute rounds separated by thirty-second breaks. A good workout consists of at least five rounds. Conditioning training can be performed on the bags, focus mitts, kicking pads, or against an imaginary opponent in shadowfighting.

The heavy bag develops power, coordination, and endurance. Here, the author unloads a series of vicious hook kicks.

Street training is the final preparation for the real thing. Most streetfights last from ten to twenty seconds, so you must prepare for this type of scenario. This means delivering explosive and powerful compound attacks with vicious intent for ten to twenty seconds, resting for one minute, and doing it again. Street training prepares you for the stress and fatigue of a real fight. It also develops power, explosiveness, speed, coordination, and distancing. You should practice this methodology in different lighting, on different surfaces, and in different surroundings. You can prepare for multiple opponents by having your training partners attack you with focus mitts arrayed in a variety of target postures. For ten to twenty seconds, go after them with vicious low-line kicks, powerful punches, and devastating strikes.

Proper mental visualization and attitude are critical to effective shadow fighting workouts. Here, the author practices the horizontal elbow strike with deep concentration and internal visualization of the shadow fighting and counter.

In the final analysis, the physical component develops a martial artist who is in maximum physical condition and armed with a brutal and deadly arsenal of tools which he can deploy with devastating results.

The Mental Component

You can equip a soldier with sophisticated weaponry, but without an intellectual grasp of warfare, he is at risk of defeat. The same principle applies to the martial artist. It is not enough to train on the physical plane—mental mastery is essential. The mental component of Contemporary Fighting Arts focuses on the cognitive development of a martial artist, including strategic development, combative mentality, cognitive exercises, philosophy, and analysis.

Strategic Development

A martial artist should never simply fight. Such a primitive approach to a dangerous situation will likely result in serious harm. Every hostile encounter is unique. Every scenario requires instantaneous assessment of various strategic factors, ranging from broad considerations such as availability of makeshift weaponry, the opponent's mind-set, somatotype, and environmental conditions (weather, floor or ground surface, lighting, escape routes, and so on), to more specific factors such as range, distancing capabilities, and the opportunity for specific tool and technique deployment.

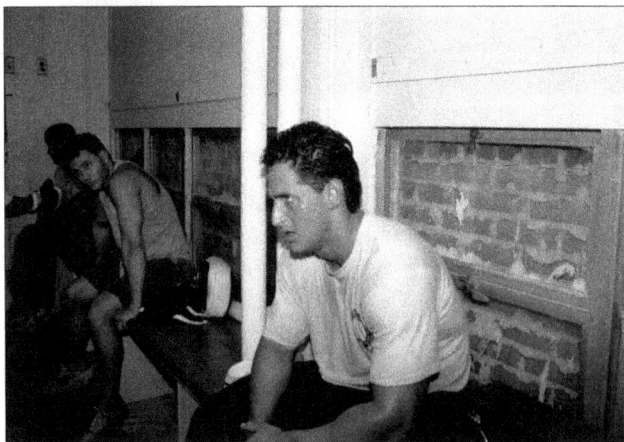

Effective training demands that students go beyond their perceived limits. Contemporary Fighting Arts classes reveal every student strengths and weaknesses.

Unarmed Combat for Street Survival

Combative Mentality

A good martial artist is a cold and dangerous animal, albeit an intelligent one. During unarmed combat, he is emotionless and calculated. He is not distracted by pain, fear, or ego, but proceeds to the task with vicious single-mindedness. This mentality results from mastery of the killer instinct. Contemporary Fighting Arts strives to develop the killer instinct in the martial artist. This combative mentality is essential for the fighter to survive the horrors of unarmed combat.

Cognitive Exercises

Contemporary Fighting Arts regularly employs cognitive exercises to enhance the martial artist's fighting skills. Mental visualization is an effective means to improve tools, techniques and maneuvers, strategic assessment, and to develop and refine the killer instinct. It is an excellent way to motivate the martial artist during grueling workouts. Mental visualization also enhances mental clarity, concentration, and emotional control.

Philosophy

Philosophical resolution of important martial issues contributes to a fighter's mental confidence and clarity. It is alarming to think of the many years spent by so many people achieving the capability to harm others, and even destroy life, with little or no time devoted to intellectual resolution of questions concerning the ultimate use of violence in defense of others and of self.

What is your purpose in studying Contemporary Fighting Arts? Why are you reading this book? What is your greatest fear? What is the source of your spiritual strength, if any? What is the mind, and what does it mean to be conscious? What is the link between mental power and physical activity? Who are you? How do you know right from wrong?

These are only a few vital questions you must resolve honestly and fully before you can advance to the highest levels of martial awareness. If you haven't begun the quest to formulate the important questions and find your answers, then take a break. It's time to figure out just why you want to know the laws and rules of unarmed combat.

Analysis

The highest level of martial mastery requires a precise and accurate understanding of how particular tools and strategies relate to various openings and ranges of unarmed combat. Every movement must be broken down to its atomic parts. The criteria of speed, power, efficiency, and destructive potential must be dissected in the context of fighting ranges. Space and time must be mastered. Analytical exercises include problem solving involving particular somatotypes aggressing in defined environments. Hypothetical opponents are moved through various ranges to facilitate insight to strategic solutions.

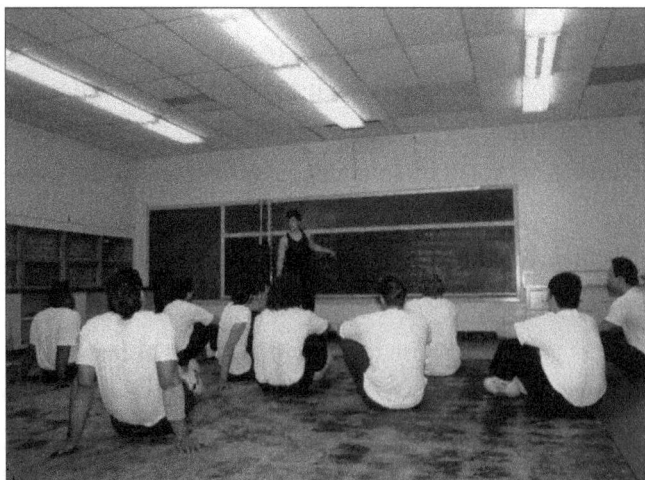

Many sessions are devoted entirely to strategic development. In this photograph, Mr. Franco lectures at the Academy.

In conjunction with problem solving sessions, practitioners are exposed to concepts of stylistic integration and modification. Oral and written examinations are given to measure the intellectual accomplishment of students. Unlike traditional systems, Contemporary Fighting Arts does not use colored belts or sashes to identify the student's level of proficiency. Instead, its ranking structure consists of colored shirts (no rank, white; rank 1, grey; rank 2, red; rank 3, blue; apprentice instructor, assistant instructor and master instructor, black). Certificates are also issued to reflect the student's level of achievement.

Contemporary Fighting Arts also studies anatomy. Understanding the physics, strengths, and weaknesses of human anatomy will greatly enhance your ability to use or abuse a body. You can drive a car without being a mechanic, but you won't understand its true limitations and tolerances unless you have some understanding of how it works.

Finally, analysis is not limited to our own system. In Contemporary Fighting Arts we seek to understand the philosophies, mentalities, strategies, training methodologies, tools, and techniques of other styles and systems.

The Spiritual Component

There are many vicious fighters. They reside in every town in every country. Some are martial artists; some are nothing more than vicious animals. I understand the deep concern of many venerable traditionalists over the abject lack of spiritual emphasis in modern combat systems. They know that you can become quite an accomplished fighter without ever mastering the self. Yet, self-mastery separates the true master from the eternal novice.

I am not referring to religious precepts or beliefs when I speak of the spiritual component. Unlike some arts, Contemporary Fighting Arts does not call upon its practitioners to merge religion into its spiritual aspect. Religion is a very personal and private matter that need not, and in my opinion should not, be incorporated into martial sciences.

So what do I mean by "spiritual component"? It is that which transcends the physical and intellectual aspects of being and reality. Ancient mystics referred to it as that which cannot be named. Whether you name it or not, it's real. There is a deeper part of each of us that is a tremendous source of truth and accomplishment.

The spiritual component of Contemporary Fighting Arts focuses on self-enlightenment. The paths to self-enlightenment are many, but the destination is singular. It is up to the martial artist to find his higher power. Universal morality, internal peace, and pure self-knowledge are the practitioner's ultimate goals.

Rectitude, dignity, honor, veracity, benevolence, loyalty. This is the moral fabric you must construct to the depths of your psyche to police and control your deadly skills. Beware—as ironic as it sounds, the more you hone these qualities the greater your capacity for destructiveness. Consider the profound knowledge underlying the creation and use of nuclear weapons. Life is not yours to give or take. This is not a religious tenet. It is a fundamental truth of the universe. If you perfect your spiritual side, you will (hopefully) never be required to use your skills. Beware of the call of violence and be ever vigilant of the ego's charms. The ego is a sly wolf desirous of destruction. Somehow, some way, you must temper and balance your lethal skills. The spiritual component of Contemporary Fighting Arts is the only true way. It is an open-ended plane of unlimited advancement.

Chapter Two
The Killer Instinct

KILLER INSTINCT

Self defense tools and techniques alone won't prepare you for the violence and other horrors of street fighting. A self defense technician must have a combative mentality to channel a destructiveness exceeding that of a deadly and evil criminal aggressor. He must be a cold and vicious animal free of fear, anger, apprehension, and ego. This mentality results from mastery of the killer instinct. Contemporary Fighting Arts (CFA) strives to develop the killer instinct in the self defense technician.

Unfortunately, some martial arts overlook this combative mentality. Many find it to be an unsavory concept unworthy of their civilized dojo or studios. In some martial art schools, the combative mentality violates their religious and philosophical beliefs. Other systems make the mistake of replacing the combative mentality with a "competitive" mentality. This sport-oriented mind set simply lacks the brutal and aggressive characteristics necessary to neutralize a crazed criminal attacker.

The killer instinct is a vest reservoir of potential he vicious energy.

Unarmed Combat for Street Survival

Everyone has a killer instinct. That's just the way it is; it's how we're made. In some it may be stronger than in others. Some manifest this instinct in gross abominations. Some never call upon it at all, but it's there. Most people manifest the killer instinct in blind rage and haphazard fury. Self-defense practitioners driven by a raw killer instinct are inferior and undisciplined warriors. Their energies are poisoned by emotion, resulting in poor body mechanics and tactical errors.

On the other hand, the self-defense practitioner who has tapped into the deep reservoir of emotional calm and mental clarity of the killer instinct can open the gates of deadly destructiveness at will. Guided by virtue and courage, one can release a most destructive energy, free of emotions. This may sound paradoxical and extreme to some. But there is, in fact, no inherent incompatibility. The advanced combat warrior must be virtuous and yet altogether capable of unleashing a controlled explosion of viciousness and brutality.

The killer instinct is predicated on being emotionless. A warrior must not experience emotions while engaged with his adversary. He must temporarily eliminate fear, anger, remorse, and ego from his conscious. Molding the average person into an emotionless warrior is not an easy task. We are, in fact, emotional creatures who, from childhood, are conditioned to feel for ourselves and others. Humans are expressive beings, crying when hurt, laughing when happy, yelling when angry. Emotional expressions are integral to our growth and development. They are, in part, the essence of humanity. It's against our nature to be otherwise. However, it's essential that the warrior remain emotionless during a violent confrontation because emotions create indecisiveness and dangerous tactical vulnerabilities.

The modern warrior must not fear death or physical disfigurement. Interestingly enough, some see fear as a positive self-defense attribute, believing the so-called "fight or flight" syndrome will help defeat the enemy. They site superhuman feats performed out of fear or panic. Perhaps the most popular one is the story of a mother who lifts a car to free her trapped child. This may or may not be possible. Frankly, I doubt it, but in any event there is no reliable correlation between rare paranormal phenomena and the deep psychological realms of unarmed combat.

Control of the emotions also prevents anger from poisoning the warrior. Anger is a useless emotion that only taxes energy and creates numerous vulnerabilities. The famous satirist Pietro Aretino put it best when he said, *"Angry men are blind and foolish, for reason at such time takes flight and, in her absence, wrath plunders all the riches of the intellect, while the judgment remains the prisoner of its own pride."*

Viciousness is another critical characteristic of the killer instinct. By viciousness I mean dangerously aggressive behavior or extreme violence. Many people will consider this the most revolting aspect of the controlled killer instinct. However, if a martial artist is to prevail in combat, he must be more vicious than his adversary. His tools and techniques must be brutal, explosive, and conclusive. At the same time, his attack must be strategically calculated to maximize efficiency, effectiveness and safety.

The killer instinct also requires a unified mind. A unified mind is one that is free from distractions and fully focused on the enemy. Distractions are derived from two sources. The first is internal, wherein your mind wanders off or panics prior to or during actual combat. The second is external, when your adversary attempts to verbally "psych you out," for example. Environmental conditions such as weather, lighting, terrain, and noise can also create external distractions. Regardless of the source, distractions must be ignored and eliminated from your consciousness.

Pain tolerance is another characteristic of the killer instinct. Pain tolerance is the ability to withstand physical pain in the midst of fighting. If a fighter is struck in combat, his mind and body must not go into shock. Pain must be familiar to you; you must keep its company well.

When harnessed, disciplined, and forged, the killer instinct is a tremendous source of power. Developing and refining this combative mentality is not an easy task. It requires the application of specific cognitive exercises, which includes visualization, meditation, and impact training.

Visualization

Through years of research and innovation I found mental visualization to be a most fascinating subject. Briefly stated, visualization is the formation of mental images to bring about desired goals ranging from improved lifestyles and health to better job performance and athletic ability.

Research indicates that mental images cause brain activity identical to that produced by an actual experience. Even if the image is unrealistic or logically impossible, the body will still produce a response that stimulates every cell in the body. There is no doubt that visualization can improve martial skills. To truly reap the benefits, however, you must make certain that your images are clear and strong. Try to feel, taste, smell, and hear the visualized scenario.

Visualization serves many purposes in Contemporary Fighting Arts. As a training aid, visualization improves tools and techniques and helps maintain motivation during grueling workouts. Visualizing strategic solutions to various street fighting altercations enhances performance. More importantly, visualization develops characteristics of the killer instinct.

Visualization is a natural and relatively simple exercise. The more often you use it the easier it becomes. Effective visualization requires a quiet place, free from distractions, for at least 20 minutes. Take the phone off the hook and tell your partner or roommate that you do not wish to be disturbed. It is vital that you have peace and quiet.

Every visualization session must be undertaken in a relaxed state, the preparatory state for visualization. To attain a state of relaxation you must first sit in a chair or lie on a couch or bed. If sitting, make certain your back is straight, your arms are uncrossed, and your feet are both on the floor. If lying down, place your arms at your side. You may want to put a pillow under your head.

Contemporary Fighting Arts uses various relaxation exercises. One of the easiest to learn is the tensing - releasing method. To begin, close your eyes and begin to breathe slowly and deeply for approximately two minutes. The next step requires you to tense every muscle in your body all at once. Clench your face and feet. Tighten your jaw and facial muscles. Tense your shoulders, chest, back, legs, and buttocks. Hold the tension for approximately ten seconds. Then in one concentrated effort, let go. Allow the tension to flow out of your body.

Visualization One

Before visualizing the killer instinct, it is important that you have a clear mental picture of yourself. Begin by visualizing yourself in a relaxed and peaceful state. Visualize your physical characteristics. Imagine your face. Note your eyes, nose, mouth, and chin. Observe the length and color of your hair. Now, look at your torso and concentrate on your chest and shoulders. See the veins that run up and down your biceps, forms, and hands. Focus on your quadriceps, hamstrings, calves, and feet. Concentrate on the clarity of the vision.

It may be helpful to glance at a picture of yourself occasionally to get a clearer image.

Now, visualize yourself in a very tranquil and pleasant environment, maybe at the park or lake. Visualize your surroundings. For example, feel the warm sun beat against your body or smell the fresh scent of pine from the beautiful trees. Remember, mental imagery is not just limited to the visual. Concentrate on crystallizing this entire scenario. This may require you to run it numerous times in your head to bring it into full focus.

Visualization Two

Visualization two deals with the environmental settings of your combative altercation. Start by visualizing yourself in a dangerous environmental setting, maybe walking through an alley in some seedy part of town. Feel the cool night air rush your body. Envision the gloomy brick buildings that surrounds you. Smell the rotten garbage as you walk past the overloaded trash cans. Listen to the sound of cars driving in the distance, hear an alley cat cry from hunger.

Now, imagine a distant figure lurking in the shadows, slowly approaching you. Mentally conjure up a person, giving him strong physical characteristics. Make him dangerous and threatening – a tall and powerful mesomorph. Begin with his facial characteristics and visualize his entire body. Smell the repulsive stench that radiates from his unbathed body. Give this imaginary criminal a motive and a voice to express it. Feel your heart accelerate and your adrenaline sore. Don't forget to visualize the essential combative factors, such as the opponent's range, positioning, and state of mine. It will be necessary to run this scenario several times in your mind to crystallize the confrontation.

Visualization Three

Visualization three deals with the manifestation of the killer instinct. In this scenario, physical violence is unavoidable, and your killer instinct is put into action. Visualize and extreme reversal in your mentality – the killer side of your temperament. Watch yourself transform into a calm, emotionless fighter. You are vicious, fearless, and free from distractions. Your mind is razor sharp and focused on your confrontation.

Visualize your chest cavity expand as oxygen fills your lungs. Hose like beans protrude from your temple, and your face begins to grin with anticipation. You are primed for violence and ready to prove it. You assume a fighting stance, and the storm of destruction begins. See yourself move forward with a brutal and vicious compound attack. The tools you choose are entirely up to you; however, be certain that they accurately relate to the circumstance, environment, range, and targets presented by the imaginary assailant. During your attack, picture the opponent's bones shatter as you deliver percussive blows. Listen to him grunt in pain and scream in agony. Finally, watch the adversary fall to the ground, incapacitated and harmless.

Try visualizing this scenario at different mental speeds. Experiment with different combative scenarios. Change the environment, circumstance, opponent, and range. Be creative, remember, no two street fights are the same, but the characteristics of the killer instinct always are.

Meditation

Meditation is a technique whereby the practitioner achieves a state of deep physiological and mental repose. It has been used throughout the centuries by the Indian yogis, Taoists, Buddhists, and mystics to achieve self-enlightenment. It generally wasn't until the 60s that Westerners recognize the value of meditation for reducing stress, muscle tension, pulse rate, high blood pressure, and other ailments.

Meditation serves many purposes and Contemporary Fighting Arts. It develops patience, inner peace, self-awareness, and a state of well-being. It also cultivates characteristics of the killer instinct. Through consistent practice you can acquire an emotional state of mind. Meditation also enhances concentration. Through its practice you learn to eliminate internal and external distractions from your mind.

Meditative postures may vary. The critical factor is to pick one that allows maximum comfort and relaxation.

Effective meditation requires a quiet environment and freedom from distractions for at least 30 minutes. A quiet and comfortable room will suffice. There is no need to burn incense or decorate your room in an oriental motif. Just keep it plain and simple. Meditation can also be practiced outdoors, as long as the location is quiet and peaceful.

Posture is another important factor. You want to be as comfortable as possible when meditating. There are many different types of meditative postures. The most common is the seated, cross leg position, wherein the legs are crossed with the feet under the thighs. The head is balanced and facing forward, the torso is erect, the hands are placed on the knees. This is by far the most comfortable and unrestricted posture. I do not recommend lying down; you should not be so relaxing your mind becomes unfocused.

Once you are in a comfortable position, close your eyes and begin to breath slowly and deeply, in through your nose and out through your mouth. The goal is to relax. The next step is the most difficult. You want to eliminate any thoughts from your mind. The objective is to remain mentally void. Don't let your mind wander or visualize. You want to reach a state of "nothingness." If thoughts and images do enter your mind, don't concentrate on them. Simply allow them to drift from your mind. Concentrating on "nothing" can be difficult and frustrating. It becomes easier with constant practice, however. If your schedule permits, meditate every day. If your time is limited, three times week will suffice. Make sure each session lasts at least 20 minutes.

Remember that results will not come overnight. It will take months, perhaps years. Like any worthwhile endeavor, meditation requires practice and time.

Impact Training

Unlike visualization and meditation, impact training is a physical exercise that develops pain tolerance. Most people fail to realize that the human body can be trained to withstand tremendous punishment and pain. Consider for example, religious fanatics who torture themselves in an attempt to reach a higher spiritual plane.

Unarmed Combat for Street Survival

In Contemporary Fighting Arts, impact training serves two purposes. On a physical level it conditions the body nerves, bones, and muscles to withstand the trauma of impact. In the rare instance that you do get hit, your body will be able to continue to fight.

On a psychological level it conditions the mind to accept and tolerate pain. In many cases, when a fighter is struck his mind goes into shock, his concentration breaks, and he panics. This is almost always leads to defeat. Impact training helps the martial artist avoid the ridiculous result of defeating himself when faced with pain.

There are two types of impact in street fighting - Snapping impact and Breaking impact. Snapping impact shocks the body but does not fully penetrate it. It is quick but lacks follow-through. For instance, a boxer's jab produces snapping impact. In contrast, breaking impact shocks and moves the body. It has maximum penetration because it follows through the target. You must be prepared to deal with both types of impact.

Impact training requires both forms of impact to be delivered to specific muscles, including the calves, thighs, abdominals, back, shoulders, chest, and arms. Striking each target will not cause any serious or permanent damage.

Warning: Under no circumstances should you strike the face, neck, throat, solar plexus, spine, groin, organs or joints. These sensitive targets cannot be conditioned to take impact, which could cause severe if not permanent injury. Therefore, it is imperative that you and your training partner be accurate when you deploy strikes and avoid these parts of the body when training.

Your training partner will also need a pair of focus mitts or boxing gloves to strike you. When he begins, it is important that he strikes lightly and slowly. Over a period of time he will be able to increase the force and speed of his strikes. Keep in mind that it will take some experimentation before you and your partner can gauge the proper amount of force. It is essential that you communicate with each other. Never feel embarrassed to tell your partner to ease up on the force.

Chapter Three
The Ranges of Unarmed Combat

One of the most important and fundamental concepts taught in Contemporary Fighting Arts is range. Briefly, range is the spatial relationship between two fighters. In unarmed combat, there are three distinct ranges in which you can engage the opponent: kicking, punching, and grappling. Prevailing in a vicious street fight requires range proficiency, or the ability to fight effectively in all three ranges of unarmed combat. Contemporary Fighting Arts is one of the few martial arts that stress this concept.

It's alarming that many popular martial arts overlook the importance of range proficiency. Consider Judo, Aikido, Wing Chun, Western Boxing, Chin-na, and certain styles of karate. While these arts might be effective in one or two ranges, they lack the tools and skills necessary to fight in all three. They are range deficient.

A range-deficient fighter is at great risk. For example, in a street fight there are many times when you can't choose the range of combat. In many instances, it is the opponent, circumstance, or environment that determines the distance.

While range proficiency is essential, certain ranges are preferred over others. However, the range you choose is not a question of personal preference, but one of efficiency, effectiveness, and overall safety. Therefore, this chapter will provide a critical analysis of the three ranges of combat by exploring the pros and cons of each range. Let's start with neutral zone.

Neutral Zone

Neutral zone is not a range of engagement. It is the distance at which neither you nor your opponent can strike each other. Neutral zone is essential for both offense and defense.

In defense, neutral zone keeps the opponent's tools from reaching you. Many opponents engage in hostile conversation prior to attacking. Many aggressors like to stand face-to-face and yell obscenities. Once his temper is heightened, the opponent will usually try to "cold cock" you with his best punch. Therefore, one of the cardinal rules of Contemporary Fighting Arts is never to remain in a range of engagement (kicking, punching, grappling) and "talk it out" with the opponent. It is simply too dangerous and risky. If the opponent wants to threaten you, let him do it from a neutral zone.

In offense, neutral zone is where your attack begins. The objective is to safely close the distance gap to kicking range. This requires a quick forward shuffle. More will be explained in chapter 4.

Neutral zone is outside any range of physical engagement. It is the only distance for conversation. Once a range of engagement is achieved, the fight must start.

The author (left) demonstrates the strategic dangers of "talking it out" in a range of engagement.

Lingering in a combat range invites the opponent to take the upper hand. Here, the attacker launches the proverbial sucker punch.

Kicking range

The farthest distance of unarmed combat is kicking range. At this distance, you are too far from the opponent to apply hand tools, so you must use your legs to strike. Northern Chinese styles, French savate, and Korean karate specialize in this range.

There are many advantages to kicking. Kicks can be delivered from a relatively safe distance and can surprise the most seasoned fighter. Compared to the arms, the legs are stronger and generate much more force. Kicks are ideal for closing the distance gap on the opponent.

There are, however, some drawbacks to kicking. Compared to the hands, the legs are slower, less accurate, and less coordinated. Balance is another factor. Whenever you raise one leg off the ground, you run the risk of losing your balance. Terrain is also a problem. Wet concrete, ice, mud, and snow are factors to consider because they may cause you to slip and fall. Kicks also require a certain amount of room to be executed successfully. Regardless of the drawbacks, however, kicks must be utilized in a street fight.

Kicking range is the distance from which any particular kicking tool can be deployed. Here, Franco demonstrates a low-line sidekick.

Kicks can be divided into two categories: high line and low-line. High line kicks are directed at targets above the opponents waist, such as the head, chest, ribs, and kidneys. Low-line kicks are directed at targets below the opponent's waist, such as the hips, groin, thigh, knee, and shin.

Unfortunately, most styles employ high-line kicks. The roundhouse, crescent, heel hook, and various spin-and-jump kicks are some of the most impressive and spectacular kicks devised. They are well-known for impressing tournament and movie audiences. However, high-line kicks pose major problems in a street fight. They are risky, and efficient, and lack the power necessary to incapacitate a powerful street aggressor.

High-line kicks drastically increase your chances of falling off balance. The ability to throw a high-line kick is also dependent upon the type of clothing you are wearing. For example, it would be difficult to execute a high-line kick if you were wearing a full-length coat, tight jeans, street clothes, or a tailored suit. Finally, high-line kicks are not as efficient as other combative tools.

High-line kicks should never be used in a real fight. They are inefficient, ineffective, and potentially dangerous for the kicker.

Contemporary Fighting Arts employees only low-line kicks. The vertical, shin, side, push, and hook kicks are safe, efficient, powerful, and very difficult to stop. All of our kicks are delivered with maximum speed and power. A kick should never "feel" or "probe" the adversary, as this would only antagonize him, prolong the encounter, and create vulnerabilities.

Low-line kicks are quick, efficient, and destructive.

In Contemporary Fighting Arts, kicks allow you to close the distance gap to punching range quickly and safely. Once this gap is closed, the martial artist can deploy the rest of a compound attack. Although kick serve primarily as entry tools to the punching range, they are frequently used to disable the opponent and create openings in his defenses.

A low-line sidekick delivers maximum destruction to vulnerable targets, yet allows the fighter to keep his balance and forward compound attack momentum.

Punching range

The mid range distance of unarmed combat is termed punching range. At this distance you are close enough to hit your opponent with your hands. Chinese Wing Chun and Western boxing are two arts that specialize in this particular range.

Punching range is the preferred range of combat in Contemporary Fighting Arts because hand tools are quick, efficient, accurate, and much safer than kicks. Hand tools do not require as much room as kicking tools. Terrain is not as much of a concern with punching as it is with kicking. While it's true that grappling range strikes are more efficient, punches are much safer. The fighter does not have to get as close to the opponent.

Punching range is just inside kicking range and is defined by the distance from which any punching tool can be deployed effectively.

Contemporary Fighting Arts does not employ punches that probe or stun the opponent. We do not advocate jabs, back fists, or overhead punches. They lack the power to neutralize a powerful aggressor. The reverse punch found in many karate styles is also inappropriate for the street. It is inefficient, slow, and leaves your centerline fully exposed. I strongly suggest eliminating these punches from your arsenal.

The punching tools of Contemporary Fighting Arts include the finger jab strike, palm heel, knife hand, lead straight, rear cross, horizontal hook, shovel hook, and uppercut. These tools are predicated on power and design to break bones. Developing accurate, bone crushing punches is not easy. It requires significant strength, controlled breathing, mastery of proper body mechanics, and years of consistent training.

Grappling range

The closest range of unarmed combat is grappling range. At this distance you are too close to the assailant to apply kicks and linear punches, so you must resort to close quarter tools and techniques. Jujitsu, Aikido, Judo, Chin-na, and wrestling are some parts that specialize in this particular range.

Grappling range is closer than punching range and is defined by the distance from which any grappling range tool can be deployed.

In street fighting, grappling range is the least preferred range. Because of your close proximity to the opponent, grappling range is risky and dangerous for the street fight. In most cases the opponent who confronts you a grappling range will want to wrestle you to the pavement. The ground is the last place you want to be in a street fight.

Unfortunately, some grappling styles focus on throws, sweeps, chokes, holds, and joint techniques rather than aggressive striking tools. However, these grappling techniques are too risky, inefficient, and impractical for street combat. Hip throws, holds, chokes, and joint locks can be negated by the opponent's strength, somatotype, state of mind, and other factors.

Many grappling holds can be countered by simple techniques. Here, Franco bites into his opponent's shoulder.

In this photo, Franco counters the opponent's hold with a thumb gouge to the eye.

Step 1: The strategic dangers of a joint lock. In this photo, the author (left) answers his opponent's initial Grab with a conventional wrist lock.

Step 2: The opponent pulls Franco into a clinch.

Unarmed Combat for Street Survival

The physical make up of the opponent also plays a big role. Consider the lunacy of applying a hold or choke to an adversary who has 100 pound weight advantage over you. Worse yet, consider the many powerful felons who spend most of their days "pumping iron" behind bars. In many cases, grappling locks and holds won't work again such powerful opponents. The opponents state of mind can nullify a joint lock. Like trapping techniques, joint locks require precise timing and exact anatomical positioning to work.

A problem arises when you are faced with an opponent who, for example, is criminally insane or high on PCP. Such an opponent will often move his arms and body frantically, disallowing any lock or hold. Furthermore, once your lock is applied there's no guarantee that it will control the assailant. I know of numerous cases where crazed men have sacrificed a broken arm or dislocated shoulder in order to free themselves from a joint lock.

Clothing is another factor. Many of the throws used in judo and jujitsu require you to grab ahold of the opponent's gi or uniform. The judo gi is constructed of heavy cotton and canvas and is designed to withstand the forceful pulling necessary for a successful throw. A problem arises, however, when you were confronted by an opponent who is shirtless or wearing a loose fitting T-shirt.

Time is another important factor to consider. A street fighting encounter should end as quickly as possible. However, chokes require sufficient time to be effective. The throat choke, which is used to slow down or cut off the blood supply to the opponent's head, can take as long as sixty seconds to produce unconsciousness. This may sound impressive; however, sixty seconds is too long in a street fight.

Contemporary Fighting Arts only employs striking tools at grappling range. Successful employment of most grappling techniques requires you to grab hold of the opponent, and most importantly, to commit to the fight. The danger occurs when your arms become preoccupied and the opponents limbs are free to counter, or when you are confronted with multiple assailants.

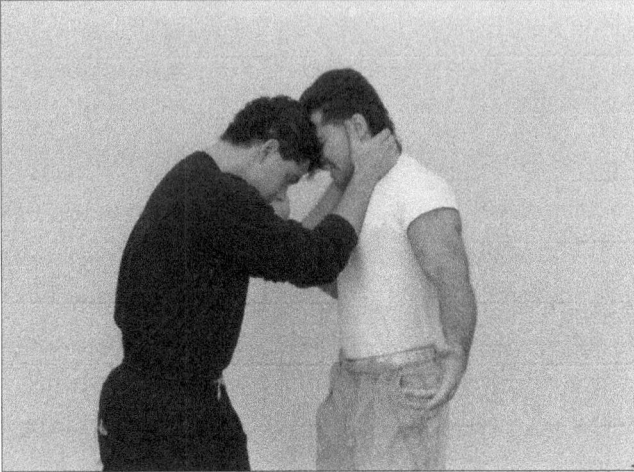

One characteristic that distinguishes Contemporary Fighting Arts from other systems is the application of striking tools at grappling range. In this photo, Franco (left) demonstrates the proper way to execute a head but strike.

Striking tools are safer and much more damaging than locks, chokes, and throws. Elbows, knees and head butts are direct, efficient, and conclusive. They can be employed against any opponent, in any state of mind. Unlike throws or joint locks, striking tools do not require you to commit yourself fully to the opponent. If a fight is taken to the pavement, there is also no need to resort to chokes her holds. Clawing, gouging, tearing, and biting are much more effective. The key is to be quick, relentless, and ruthless.

Trapping range

Trapping range is the distance between punching range and grappling range. At this distance, you are close enough to immobilize the opponent's hands. Trapping techniques are found in styles such as Chinese Wing Chun, Praying Mantis Kung-Fu, and Filipino Kali.

Trapping momentarily controls the opponents arms, allowing you to execute an offensive attack. Trapping also draws reactions from the opponent, allowing you to counter. However, in Contemporary Fighting Arts, we do not advocate trapping and, therefore, do not acknowledge a trapping range. There are simply too many uncertainties and variables involved in trapping.

Trapping range is just between punching and graphing range. Notice the attachment of the hands.

Trapping is dependent on the opponent presenting certain variables and responses. For example, if your trapping feed are not adequately engaged by the opponent, you can't build a trapping structure. If the opponent disengages, which is extremely likely in a street fight, the trap disintegrates. Worse yet, the assailant can move to grappling range easily and quickly and utilize a series of head butts, elbows, and knee strikes. Trapping too often results in a wrestling situation, which invariably ends up on the ground. This is the last place you want to be in a street fight. More will be explained in chapter 5.

Today's martial artist must be capable of fighting in all three combat ranges – kicking, punching and grappling. In this confrontation Franco (center) employees both kicking and punching tools.

Chapter Four
Range Manipulation

Strategy is all important in combat. From the great battles of antiquity to modern wars, strategy has been the dominant force in successful military encounters. King David, Attila the Hun, Sun Tzu, Napoleon, and Patton are but a few who have demonstrated the significance of strategic warfare. Brilliant tacticians will be remembered and honored always.

Information on large-scale military strategies is overwhelming. Libraries and bookstores are filled with thousands of books on the subject. Surprisingly, however, there is little literature on strategy of individualize combat. Strategy is one of the most important factors in street fighting, yet it has been overlooked. The probability of a one-on-one confrontation is far greater than a large-scale war. Attacks occur daily, and there is a vital necessity for individualized combat strategy.

In Contemporary Fighting Arts, strategy is viewed as both a science and an art. It is the bedrock of preparedness. In street fighting, strategic preparedness can make the difference between life and death. When confronted by overwhelming forces (e.g., 250-pound psychopathic mesomorph or multiple opponents), it can even the odds. Movements become more efficient and effective. The risk of mistake or injury is greatly reduced. In general, strategic solutions to violent encounters enhance your chances of victory.

Consider the many strategists who advocate"probes" and "feelers" to assess the opponent's style, reaction time, conditioning, and overall combative abilities. This may sound effective, but in a street fight it is simply too risky. Who has time to assess the opponents skill in a fight? By the time an assessment is made, the altercation will be over. One should never design a strategy or conduct experiments in the midst of combat. A motto of Contemporary Fighting Arts is, "Experimentation in the face of danger is an invitation to disaster."

One strategy that has proved is effectiveness time and time again is range manipulation. Briefly, range manipulation is the skillful and strategic exploitation of ranges for both offense of an defensive purposes. Range manipulation requires quick, non-telegraphic movement, intuitive tool response, and extensive target orientation.

Mobility is also essential in range manipulation. Quick and efficient movement is accomplished through basic footwork. Footwork means quick, economical steps performed on the balls of the feet, while remaining relaxed and balanced. In Contemporary Fighting Arts, basic footwork is structured around the following for movements:

Moving forward - from your fighting stance, first move your front foot forward (approximately 12 inches) and then move your rear foot an equal distance.

Moving backward - from your fighting stance, first move your rear foot backward (approximately 12 inches) and then move your front foot an equal distance.

Sidestepping right - from your fighting stance, first move your right foot to the right (approximately 12 inches) and then move your left foot an equal distance.

Sidestepping left - from your fighting stance, first move your left foot to the left (approximately 12 inches) and then move your right foot an equal distance.

Offensive Range Manipulation

The objective of offensive range manipulation is to move explosively through the ranges of combat while delivering an overwhelming compound attack. Your attack begins from the neutral zone and ends in punching range. Once in punching range, deliver a flurry of full-force, full-speed punches. The trick is to get to punching range and stay there. This may sound easy, but I assure you that it is not. It requires quick, non-telegraphic movement, precise timing, and excellent footwork. The following principles are vital to offensive range manipulation.

- From a neutral zone, close the gap to kicking range with a powerful low-line kick. When your kick hits, explode into punching range. Proceed with a flurry of full-force, full-speed blows. Make certain that your tools are appropriate to the opponent's targets.

- Remain and punching range and keep the pressure on. Stay defensively alert, however, since many opponents will swing wildly or charge forward in a last act of desperation.

- If the opponent moves into grappling range, immediately employee grappling strikes with the same overwhelming speed as your punches. Don't let the opponent break the offensive flow. Continue until the assailant is neutralized.

- If the opponent retreats to kicking range, immediately respond with a low-line kick and explode to punching range. Continue with punching tools. Keep the pressure on until the opponent is neutralized. Once the adversary is incapacitated, move back to neutral zone.

Defensive Range Manipulation

Although street fighting should be approach offensively, there are certain instances in which the martial artist must resort to defensive skills. When faced with a singular kick, punch, or strike, you will almost always respond with a block, parry, or slipping maneuver. However, when confronted with an overwhelming compound attack, defensive range manipulation is your only chance.

Unarmed Combat for Street Survival

A compound attack is simply too fast and powerful to block, parry, or slip. Coordinating blocking, parrying, and slipping maneuvers for a vicious compound attack is absurd, not to mention impossible. When you are faced with a flurry of blows, defensive range manipulation allows you to disengage the opponent's compound attack quickly and safely so you can counter the assault.

Let me emphasize that street fighting should never be approached defensively. To prevail in a street fight, you must take the initiative and strike first. Having said that, let's look at the key principles of defense range manipulation.

- When the opponent rushes you with an overwhelming compound attack, do not attempt to block, parry or slip the flurry. Immediately retreat from punching range to kicking range. This can be accomplished with a quick backward shuffle.

- Once in kicking range, simultaneously counter with a lowline kick. Be certain that your kick is accurate, powerful, and properly timed.

- Once your kick hits its target, explode to punching range. Proceed with your own flurry of full-speed, full-force blows.

- Keep the pressure on until the opponent is neutralized. Once he is incapacitated, move back to neutral zone.

KILLER INSTINCT

Chapter Five
The Methods of Attack

Defense is a fundamental concept found in every martial art. In some systems it's a foundational philosophy; in others it's a strategic approach to combat. For example, most instructors, both traditional and modern, stress defensive responses rather than offensive action in a violent encounter. It's also interesting that most katas begin and end with a block, illustrating the defensive attitude of most karate styles. Defense is, without a doubt, the staple of most conventional fighting systems.

Unfortunately, defensive approaches to street fighting can be disastrous. The martial artist who approaches street fighting defensively runs the risk of severe injury or even death. Allowing the opponent the first move is absolutely insane; it's like allowing a gunslinger the first draw. Most violent confrontations are won by the fighter who initiates. It's that simple.

Unlike conventional systems, Contemporary Fighting Arts is predicated on offense. If combat is unavoidable, the martial artist must take the initiative and strike first, fast and with authority. You must accept this offense of philosophy and master the art of attack if you are to prevail in a brutal street fight.

Today, most modernist acknowledge five basic methods of attack. These methods are generally considered the strategic norm, and they are classified as follows:

- **Attack by drawing**
- **Immobilization attack**
- **Indirect attack**
- **Single attack**
- **Compound attack**

Attack by Drawing

Attack by drawing is counter fighting. In this method of attack, the martial artist offers the opponent an enticing bait (i.e. an intentional opening designed to lure an attack). A common drawing technique is wide hand positioning, as if to say, "Come on, take your best shot!"

Once the opponent takes the bait, the practitioner swiftly executes a preplanned and perfectly timed counter attack. Proponents of this attack method argue that it forces the opponent to commit himself to a decided action and offers you the opportunity to observe his style of fighting.

While the Attack by Drawing (ABD) method may be safe to use under sparring conditions, it poses dangerous problems in a real fight. In such a dangerous situation, who's to say you'll be able to stop, intercept or counter the opponent's initial attack. For example, suppose he has exceptional hand speed. Or, what if the adversary seizes your intentional opening as an opportunity to initiate a deceptive and relentless flurry of devastating blows? You could easily find yourself in an irreversible defensive flow that could get you severely injured or possibly killed in the streets.

The bottom line is under no circumstances should you allow the opponent to gain the advantage of initiating the first strike in a real fight. Frankly, it's like allowing a gunslinger to draw his weapon first. If he's accurate and hits his target, it's light out for you!

Once it is clear that you will be attacked, or that a fight is unavoidable, you should do everything in your power to take control the situation. This means strike first, strike fast, strike with authority, and keep the pressure on.

The following two photos demonstrate the dangers of drawing. Here, Franco squares off with his opponent and assumes a wide hand positioning to draw an attack.

Here, the opponent exploits Franco's opening with a quick strike to the chin.

Unarmed Combat for Street Survival

This offensive strategy is known as my first-strike principle, and it's essential to the process of neutralizing a formidable adversary in a high-risk self-defense altercation. A first strike is defined as the strategic application of proactive force designed to interrupt the initial stages of an assault before it becomes a full-blown self-defense situation.

One inescapable fact about street self-defense is that the longer the fight lasts, the greater your chances of serious injury or even death. Common sense suggests that you must end the fight as quickly as possible. Striking first is the best method of achieving this tactical objective because it permits you to neutralize your assailant swiftly while, at the same time, precluding his ability to retaliate effectively. No time is wasted, and no unnecessary risks are taken.

When it comes to reality based self-defense, the element of surprise is invaluable. Launching the first strike gives you the upper hand because it allows you to hit the adversary suddenly and unexpectedly. As a result, you demolish his defenses and ultimately take him out of the fight.

Ultimately, the best defense is a powerful and overwhelming offense. I agree that deception is a key factor in all forms of combat, however, the attack by drawing method (ABD) is a gamble you should never take on the street.

Immobilization Attack

Immobilization Attack, also called trapping, is a highly complex system of moves and counter moves designed to control the opponent's limb(s) in order to execute an offense attack. Trapping techniques may be applied against arms, hands or legs. Generally, however, the more intricate trapping techniques involve the upper gates, i.e., the arms and hands. Trapping requires lightning-quick reflexes and highly developed tactile sensitivity. It truly is an impressive sight to watch two really accomplish trappers go at it. However, aesthetics do not dictate the outcome of the vicious and potentially deadly street fight.

Effective trapping techniques are based on the opponent presenting a proper structure for response. His hands must accept the trappers initiating feed in just the right way. The trapping feed can either be a linear or circular attack to engage the opponent's counter or guard. Once the initial lockup takes place the trapper can go to work with close-quarter strikes, parries, locks, energy reversals and other techniques aimed at neutralizing the opponent and gaining further openings. All of this may sound impressive but for the street it can be disastrous. As I said before, just because this method of attack worked for Bruce Lee, doesn't necessarily mean it will work for you.

The truth is you simply cannot rely on your opponent presenting the predefined structure necessary for various trapping techniques. For example, if your "feeds" are not adequately engaged by the opponent, you can't build a trapping structure. If the opponent disengages - which is extremely likely in a real fighting situation - the trap disintegrates. Worse yet, the opponent can easily counter the lockup with a series of head butts, elbows, knee strikes and body tackles.

Some proponents of trapping argue that it's a by-product of hitting. They say that you should hit before and after every trap, and you should only trap when your strike is obstructed. However, in the real world, combat is frenzied and unpredictable. In some ways, it's likened to a gruesome car wreck. In almost all cases your adversary will be fueled by blood-thirsty rage and pure adrenaline. He simply won't offer you the static and controlled defensive structure necessary for effective trapping techniques.

There are simply too many uncertainties and variables to trapping. These techniques are based on assumptions you cannot afford to make in a high risk self-defense situation. Finally, trapping too often results in a grappling situation which invariably ends up on the ground. This is the last place you want to be in a street fight. The bottom line is – leave trapping in the gym or dojo. Don't take it to the streets.

Here, the author squares off with his opponent. This sequence of photographs demonstrate the inherent complexity of trapping techniques and the need for appropriate responses by the opponent.

Here, Franco demonstrates the attachment, assuming his opponent will respond as anticipated.

Once engaged with the opponent, Franco builds on the trap with a slap block (pak sao) and a lead vertical punch.

Once the opponent's parrying hand crosses the centerline, Franco then grabs (lop sao) the opponent's rear hand and counters with a back fist.

Indirect Attack

The indirect attack is progressive in nature. It always involves more than one offense technique. Do not, however, confuse the indirect attack with its superior cousin, the compound attack.

The indirect attack builds through stages. The initial techniques is not the coup de grace, i.e., the knockout weapon. In fact, in many indirect attacks the initiating technique is not even the weapon, but one of any number of feints or other deceptions designed to open the opponent up for the follow-up blow. Even when the initial technique is an actual kick, punch or any other striking tool, it serves merely as a set-up for the finishing blow.

In competition, the initiating technique sets up or accumulates valuable points, wears down the opponent, and opens them up to more devastating blows. The progressive indirect attack can also be very effective under sparring conditions. In real combat, however, where points are of no consequence and setups are not safe, the progressive indirect attack should not be employed.

In the explosive and dangerous situation of a real street fight, the martial artist cannot afford the risk of a setup technique. Any initiating strike delivered with less than maximum speed and force may likely be ignored and will certainly be countered with viciousness. Consider the sheer lunacy of attempting a feint against an opponent such as professional boxer. You cannot afford to gamble that your adversary will react in the manner intended.

Those who have trained excessively in the use of feints, should limit their use to closing the distance gap from a neutral distance. A feint from the neutral range does not create a risk as it would in any of the three ranges of unarmed combat. If the opponent fails to take the bait or reacts offensively, you're still at a relatively safe distance. Never use a feint in a range of engagement, i.e., kicking, punching, or grappling range. Feints from these ranges run the risk of an offense counter allowing the opponent to get the upper hand and thereby placing you in the defensive flow.

Simply put, assumptions and experimentation in the face of danger are invitations to disaster! The progressive indirect attack involves too much risk and uncertainty. It lacks the all-out explosiveness, power and commitment required in the face of an attack by an opponent hell-bent on your destruction. Remember, in a high-risk self-defense situation no rules apply. Your subject to an attack from anywhere and anything. You cannot allow a dangerous assailant even the slightest opportunity get the upper hand.

Step 1: Franco squares off with his adversary.

Step 2: Franco begins his indirect attack with a low feint. His opponent goes for the feint by parrying down with his left hand. Notice how Franco exposes his head to his opponent.

Step 3: Fortunately, his assumptions bear out. Franco completes his indirect attack with a right hook to the opening.

The risks of the indirect attack are many. Here, Franco squares off with his adversary.

Franco begins his indirect attack with a low feint. His opponent quickly counters with a lead straight.

Single Attack

The single attack is also called the simple direct attack (SDA). In this method, the martial artist delivers a solitary offense technique. It may involve a series of discrete probes or one swift and powerful strike aimed at terminating the encounter. Whatever the strategy, the simple angle attack and simple direct attack is predicated entirely upon one isolated strike.

Some proponents of this method argue that it is the safest attack because it does not require full commitment to the opponent. Others proclaim it to be the highest form of attack when one swift, powerful blow dictates the outcome of the fight.

First, in a real fight, what possible sense does it make to remain uncommitted to the adversary? The fact is, you cannot effectively neutralize a formidable aggressor by lingering at the perimeter of the encounter. Rather than toying with probes and other isolated "feelers," you must commit yourself 100% with the most powerful and effective flow of tools appropriate to the targets, ranges, and openings.

In this photo, Franco attempts to end the altercation with one swift kick.

Once Franco completes his kick, the opponent rushes in with a rear cross. One-strike victories are few and far between.

Furthermore, you cannot afford the risk that one perfectly executed punch, palm heel strike, kick or other technique will terminate the fight. It's not that it can't be done. It's just that single strike victories are few and far between. They are the rare luxury of the highly trained and skilled martial artist – and even then, it sometimes requires a little luck.

To drive the point home, think of the now familiar law enforcement stories of drug-induced criminal aggressors who keep coming after being hit by a .38 caliber bullet. There are a lot of those types of people out there and they're often involved in violent street attacks.

The bottom line is, unless you are Bruce Lee, you cannot rely on the simple attack to stop such a dangerous assailant. In almost every case you won't know your aggressor's pain tolerance, state of mind or capability for violence.

However, there's nothing wrong with developing the capability to knock your opponent out with a single blow. In fact, every serious martial artist should have a few knock-out techniques in his or her arsenal. Here are a few ways you can develop bone-shattering power.

Compound Attack

Attack by combination is also called a compound attack. A compound attack is any sequence of two or more tools launched in succession. However, it is significantly different from all the other methods of attack. It does not build through progressive stages; no time is wasted, and no unnecessary risks are taken.

Attack by combination has nothing to do with experimentation or assumptions. Rather, the martial artist gains the upper hand by initiating a flurry of strategically placed full-force, full-speed strikes designed to overwhelm the opponent's defenses. The ultimate objective is to take the fight out to the opponent and the opponent out of the fight.

Based on power, accuracy, speed and commitment, the compound attack also requires calculation, control and clarity. In other words, the unskilled, untrained brawler who goes off with a buzzsaw of violent strikes is not executing a compound attack. There is more to it than that.

The compound attack starts with a thorough understanding and knowledge of every conceivable anatomical target presented by the various stances, angles, distances, and movements of the opponent. Unless he is in full body armor, there are always targets. It is a question of recognizing them and striking quickly with the appropriate tools. This requires mastery of a wide range of offensive techniques, a complete understanding of combat ranges, reaction dynamic awareness, and the proper use of force.

Contemporary Fighting Arts employs only the compound attack. In this photo, Franco closes the distance gap with a sidekick to the opponent's knee.

Franco immediately identifies a second target and initiates a powerful rear cross punch.

He follows through with an elbow strike.

The compound attack is completed with a knee strike. Remember that each tool is executed with full speed, power, and commitment.

But remember, what is universally true for all opponents is equally true for you. If there is always a target available on him, there's always one on you – although vulnerability can be reduced with proper martial arts training. Remember, strike first, strike fast, strike with authority, and keep the pressure on.

As you attack one target, others open up naturally. It is up to you to recognize them through reaction dynamic awareness and keep the offensive flow. Executed properly, the compound attack demolishes your opponents defenses that you ultimately take him down and out. It sounds great, but you must realize that it has to happen within seconds.

You cannot train enough in the compound method of attack. The martial artist must always focus on power and relentless directness. In Contemporary Fighting Arts, we believe the truth in offense rests in the compound attack. It is efficient, effective, safe and destructive. When the chips are down, it's your only sure chance.

Unarmed Combat for Street Survival

KILLER INSTINCT

Conclusion

Contemporary Fighting Arts is a synthesis of the physical, mental, and spiritual elements of unarmed combat. Its goal is to train artists in the most efficient and effective tools and techniques for a game where no rules apply. Imparting this knowledge of destructiveness carries with it a tremendous responsibility, and Contemporary Fighting Arts insists that its practitioners adhere to the highest virtues and tenets of social responsibility. Contemporary Fighting Arts' vision of martial truth is to produce modern moral warriors individually responsible for their survival.

For more information regarding Contemporary Fighting Arts, please visit our website at: **SammyFranco.com**

KILLER INSTINCT

Glossary

The following terms are defined in the context of Contemporary Fighting Arts and its related concepts. In many instances, the definitions bear little resemblance to those found in a standard dictionary.

A

accuracy—The precise or exact projection of force. Accuracy is also defined as the ability to execute a combative movement with precision and exactness.

adaptability—The ability to physically and psychologically adjust to new or different conditions or circumstances of combat.

advanced first-strike tools—Offensive techniques that are specifically used when confronted with multiple opponents.

aerobic exercise—Literally, "with air." Exercise that elevates the heart rate to a training level for a prolonged period of time, usually 30 minutes.

affective preparedness – One of the three components of preparedness. Affective preparedness means being emotionally, philosophically, and spiritually prepared for the strains of combat. See cognitive preparedness and psychomotor preparedness.

aggression—Hostile and injurious behavior directed toward a person.

aggressive response—One of the three possible counters when assaulted by a grab, choke, or hold from a standing position. Aggressive response requires you to counter the enemy with destructive blows and strikes. See moderate response and passive response.

aggressive hand positioning—Placement of hands so as to imply aggressive or hostile intentions.

agility—An attribute of combat. One's ability to move his or her body quickly and gracefully.

amalgamation—A scientific process of uniting or merging.

ambidextrous—The ability to perform with equal facility on both the right and left sides of the body.

anabolic steroids – synthetic chemical compounds that resemble the male sex hormone testosterone. This performance-enhancing drug is known to increase lean muscle mass, strength, and endurance.

analysis and integration—One of the five elements of CFA's mental component. This is the painstaking process of breaking down various elements, concepts, sciences, and disciplines into their atomic parts, and then methodically and strategically analyzing, experimenting, and drastically modifying the information so that it fulfills three combative requirements: efficiency, effectiveness, and safety. Only then is it finally integrated into the CFA system.

anatomical striking targets—The various anatomical body targets that can be struck and which are especially vulnerable to potential harm. They include: the eyes, temple, nose, chin, back of neck, front of neck, solar plexus, ribs, groin, thighs, knees, shins, and instep.

anchoring – The strategic process of trapping the assailant's neck or limb in order to control the range of engagement during razing.

assailant—A person who threatens or attacks another person.

assault—The threat or willful attempt to inflict injury upon the person of another.

assault and battery—The unlawful touching of another person without justification.

assessment—The process of rapidly gathering, analyzing, and accurately evaluating information in terms of threat and danger. You can assess people, places, actions, and objects.

attack—Offensive action designed to physically control, injure, or kill another person.

attack by combination (ABC) - One of the five methods of attack. See compound attack.

attack by drawing (ABD) - One of the five methods of attack. A method of attack predicated on counterattack.

attitude—One of the three factors that determine who wins a street fight. Attitude means being emotionally, philosophically, and spiritually liberated from societal and religious mores. See skills and knowledge.

attributes of combat—The physical, mental, and spiritual qualities that enhance combat skills and tactics.

awareness—Perception or knowledge of people, places, actions, and objects. (In CFA, there are three categories of tactical awareness: criminal awareness, situational awareness, and self-awareness.)

B

balance—One's ability to maintain equilibrium while stationary or moving.

blading the body—Strategically positioning your body at a 45-degree angle.

blitz and disengage—A style of sparring whereby a fighter moves into a range of combat, unleashes a strategic compound attack, and then quickly disengages to a safe distance. Of all sparring methodologies, the blitz and disengage most closely resembles a real street fight.

block—A defensive tool designed to intercept the assailant's attack by placing a non-vital target between the assailant's strike and your vital body target.

body composition—The ratio of fat to lean body tissue.

body language—Nonverbal communication through posture, gestures, and facial expressions.

body mechanics—Technically precise body movement during the execution of a body weapon, defensive technique, or other fighting maneuver.

body tackle – A tackle that occurs when your opponent haphazardly rushes forward and plows his body into yours.

body weapon—Also known as a tool, one of the various body parts that can be used to strike or otherwise injure or kill a criminal assailant.

burn out—A negative emotional state acquired by physically over- training. Some symptoms include: illness, boredom, anxiety, disinterest in training, and general sluggishness.

C

cadence—Coordinating tempo and rhythm to establish a timing pattern of movement.

cardiorespiratory conditioning—The component of physical fitness that deals with the heart, lungs, and circulatory system.

centerline—An imaginary vertical line that divides your body in half and which contains many of your vital anatomical targets.

choke holds—Holds that impair the flow of blood or oxygen to the brain.

circular movements—Movements that follow the direction of a curve.

close-quarter combat—One of the three ranges of knife and

bludgeon combat. At this distance, you can strike, slash, or stab your assailant with a variety of close-quarter techniques.

cognitive development—One of the five elements of CFA's mental component. The process of developing and enhancing your fighting skills through specific mental exercises and techniques. See analysis and integration, killer instinct, philosophy, and strategic/tactical development.

cognitive exercises—Various mental exercises used to enhance fighting skills and tactics.

cognitive preparedness – One of the three components of preparedness. Cognitive preparedness means being equipped with the strategic concepts, principles, and general knowledge of combat. See affective preparedness and psychomotor preparedness.

combat-oriented training—Training that is specifically related to the harsh realities of both armed and unarmed combat. See ritual-oriented training and sport-oriented training.

combative arts—The various arts of war. See martial arts.

combative attributes—See attributes of combat.

combative fitness—A state characterized by cardiorespiratory and muscular/skeletal conditioning, as well as proper body composition.

combative mentality—Also known as the killer instinct, this is a combative state of mind necessary for fighting. See killer instinct.

combat ranges—The various ranges of unarmed combat.

combative utility—The quality of condition of being combatively useful.

combination(s)—See compound attack.

common peroneal nerve—A pressure point area located approximately four to six inches above the knee on the midline of the outside of the thigh.

composure—A combative attribute. Composure is a quiet and focused mind-set that enables you to acquire your combative agenda.

compound attack—One of the five conventional methods of attack. Two or more body weapons launched in strategic succession whereby the fighter overwhelms his assailant with a flurry of full speed, full-force blows.

conditioning training—A CFA training methodology requiring the practitioner to deliver a variety of offensive and defensive combinations for a 4-minute period. See proficiency training and street training.

contact evasion—Physically moving or manipulating your body to avoid being tackled by the adversary.

Contemporary Fighting Arts—A modern martial art and self-defense system made up of three parts: physical, mental, and spiritual.

conventional ground-fighting tools—Specific ground-fighting techniques designed to control, restrain, and temporarily incapacitate your adversary. Some conventional ground fighting tactics include: submission holds, locks, certain choking techniques, and specific striking techniques.

coordination—A physical attribute characterized by the ability to perform a technique or movement with efficiency, balance, and accuracy.

counterattack—Offensive action made to counter an assailant's initial attack.

courage—A combative attribute. The state of mind and spirit that enables a fighter to face danger and vicissitudes with confidence, resolution, and bravery.

creatine monohydrate—A tasteless and odorless white powder that mimics some of the effects of anabolic steroids. Creatine is a safe body-building product that can benefit anyone who wants to increase their strength, endurance, and lean muscle mass.

criminal awareness—One of the three categories of CFA awareness. It involves a general understanding and knowledge of the nature and dynamics of a criminal's motivations, mentalities, methods, and capabilities to perpetrate violent crime. See situational awareness and self-awareness.

criminal justice—The study of criminal law and the procedures associated with its enforcement.

criminology—The scientific study of crime and criminals.

cross-stepping—The process of crossing one foot in front of or behind the other when moving.

crushing tactics—Nuclear grappling-range techniques designed to crush the assailant's anatomical targets.

D

deadly force—Weapons or techniques that may result in unconsciousness, permanent disfigurement, or death.

deception—A combative attribute. A stratagem whereby you delude your assailant.

decisiveness—A combative attribute. The ability to follow a tactical course of action that is unwavering and focused.

defense—The ability to strategically thwart an assailant's attack (armed or unarmed).

defensive flow—A progression of continuous defensive responses.

defensive mentality—A defensive mind-set.

defensive reaction time—The elapsed time between an assailant's physical attack and your defensive response to that attack. See offensive reaction time.

demeanor—A person's outward behavior. One of the essential factors to consider when assessing a threatening individual.

diet—A lifestyle of healthy eating.

disingenuous vocalization—The strategic and deceptive utilization of words to successfully launch a preemptive strike at your adversary.

distancing—The ability to quickly understand spatial relationships and how they relate to combat.

distractionary tactics—Various verbal and physical tactics designed to distract your adversary.

double-end bag—A small leather ball hung from the ceiling and anchored to the floor with bungee cord. It helps develop striking accuracy, speed, timing, eye-hand coordination, footwork and overall defensive skills.

double-leg takedown—A takedown that occurs when your opponent shoots for both of your legs to force you to the ground.

E

ectomorph—One of the three somatotypes. A body type characterized by a high degree of slenderness, angularity, and fragility. See endomorph and mesomorph.

effectiveness—One of the three criteria for a CFA body weapon, technique, tactic, or maneuver. It means the ability to produce a desired effect. See efficiency and safety.

efficiency—One of the three criteria for a CFA body weapon, technique, tactic, or maneuver. It means the ability to reach an objective quickly and economically. See effectiveness and safety.

emotionless—A combative attribute. Being temporarily devoid of human feeling.

endomorph—One of the three somatotypes. A body type characterized by a high degree of roundness, softness, and body fat. See ectomorph and mesomorph.

evasion—A defensive maneuver that allows you to strategically maneuver your body away from the assailant's strike.

evasive sidestepping—Evasive footwork where the practitioner moves to either the right or left side.

evasiveness—A combative attribute. The ability to avoid threat or danger.

excessive force—An amount of force that exceeds the need for a particular event and is unjustified in the eyes of the law.

experimentation—The painstaking process of testing a combative hypothesis or theory.

explosiveness—A combative attribute that is characterized by a sudden outburst of violent energy.

F

fear—A strong and unpleasant emotion caused by the anticipation or awareness of threat or danger. There are three stages of fear in order of intensity: fright, panic, and terror. See fright, panic, and terror.

feeder—A skilled technician who manipulates the focus mitts.

femoral nerve—A pressure point area located approximately 6 inches above the knee on the inside of the thigh.

fighting stance—Any one of the stances used in CFA's system. A strategic posture you can assume when face-to-face with an unarmed assailant(s). The fighting stance is generally used after you have launched your first-strike tool.

fight-or-flight syndrome—A response of the sympathetic nervous system to a fearful and threatening situation, during which it prepares your body to either fight or flee from the perceived danger.

finesse—A combative attribute. The ability to skillfully execute a movement or a series of movements with grace and refinement.

first strike—Proactive force used to interrupt the initial stages of an assault before it becomes a self-defense situation.

first-strike principle—A CFA principle that states that when physical danger is imminent and you have no other tactical option but to fight back, you should strike first, strike fast, and strike with authority and keep the pressure on.

first-strike stance—One of the stances used in CFA's system. A strategic posture used prior to initiating a first strike.

first-strike tools—Specific offensive tools designed to initiate a preemptive strike against your adversary.

fisted blows – Hand blows delivered with a clenched fist.

five tactical options – The five strategic responses you can make in a self-defense situation, listed in order of increasing level of resistance: comply, escape, de-escalate, assert, and fight back.

flexibility—The muscles' ability to move through maximum natural ranges. See muscular/skeletal conditioning.

focus mitts—Durable leather hand mitts used to develop and sharpen offensive and defensive skills.

footwork—Quick, economical steps performed on the balls of the feet while you are relaxed, alert, and balanced. Footwork is structured around four general movements: forward, backward, right, and left.

fractal tool—Offensive or defensive tools that can be used in more than one combat range.

fright—The first stage of fear; quick and sudden fear. See panic and terror.

full Beat – One of the four beat classifications in the Widow Maker Program. The full beat strike has a complete initiation and retraction phase.

G

going postal - a slang term referring to a person who suddenly and unexpectedly attacks you with an explosive and frenzied flurry of blows. Also known as postal attack.

grappling range—One of the three ranges of unarmed combat. Grappling range is the closest distance of unarmed combat from which you can employ a wide variety of close-quarter tools and techniques. The grappling range of unarmed combat is also divided into two planes: vertical (standing) and horizontal (ground fighting). See kicking range and punching range.

grappling-range tools—The various body tools and techniques that are employed in the grappling range of unarmed combat, including head butts; biting, tearing, clawing, crushing, and gouging tactics; foot stomps, horizontal, vertical, and diagonal elbow strikes, vertical and diagonal knee strikes, chokes, strangles, joint locks, and holds. See punching range tools and kicking range tools.

ground fighting—Also known as the horizontal grappling plane, this is fighting that takes place on the ground.

guard—Also known as the hand guard, this refers to a fighter's hand positioning.

guard position—Also known as leg guard or scissors hold, this is a ground-fighting position in which a fighter is on his back holding his opponent between his legs.

H

half beat – One of the four beat classifications in the Widow Maker Program. The half beat strike is delivered through the retraction phase of the proceeding strike.

hand immobilization attack (HIA) - One of the five methods of attack. A method of attack whereby the practitioner traps his opponent's limb or limbs in order to execute an offense attack of his own.

hand positioning—See guard.

hand wraps—Long strips of cotton that are wrapped around the hands and wrists for greater protection.

haymaker—A wild and telegraphed swing of the arms executed by an unskilled fighter.

head-hunter—A fighter who primarily attacks the head.

heavy bag—A large cylindrical bag used to develop kicking, punching, or striking power.

high-line kick—One of the two different classifications of a kick. A kick that is directed to targets above an assailant's waist level. See low-line kick.

hip fusing—A full-contact drill that teaches a fighter to "stand his ground" and overcome the fear of exchanging blows with a stronger opponent. This exercise is performed by connecting two fighters with a 3-foot chain, forcing them to fight in the punching range of unarmed combat.

histrionics—The field of theatrics or acting.

hook kick—A circular kick that can be delivered in both kicking and punching ranges.

hook punch—A circular punch that can be delivered in both the punching and grappling ranges.

I

impact power—Destructive force generated by mass and velocity.

impact training—A training exercise that develops pain tolerance.

incapacitate—To disable an assailant by rendering him unconscious or damaging his bones, joints, or organs.

initiative—Making the first offensive move in combat.

inside position—The area between the opponent's arms, where he has the greatest amount of control.

intent—One of the essential factors to consider when assessing a threatening individual. The assailant's purpose or motive. See demeanor, positioning, range, and weapon capability.

intuition—The innate ability to know or sense something without the use of rational thought.

J

jeet kune do (JKD) - "Way of the intercepting fist." Bruce Lee's approach to the martial arts, which includes his innovative concepts, theories, methodologies, and philosophies.

jersey Pull - Strategically pulling the assailant's shirt or jacket over his head as he disengages from the clinch position.

joint lock—A grappling-range technique that immobilizes the assailant's joint.

K

kick—A sudden, forceful strike with the foot.

kicking range—One of the three ranges of unarmed combat. Kicking range is the furthest distance of unarmed combat wherein you use your legs to strike an assailant. See grappling range and punching range.

kicking-range tools—The various body weapons employed in the kicking range of unarmed combat, including side kicks, push kicks, hook kicks, and vertical kicks.

killer instinct—A cold, primal mentality that surges to your consciousness and turns you into a vicious fighter.

kinesics—The study of nonlinguistic body movement communications. (For example, eye movement, shrugs, or facial gestures.)

kinesiology—The study of principles and mechanics of human movement.

kinesthetic perception—The ability to accurately feel your body during the execution of a particular movement.

knowledge—One of the three factors that determine who will win a street fight. Knowledge means knowing and understanding how to fight. See skills and attitude.

L

lead side -The side of the body that faces an assailant.

leg guard—See guard position.

linear movement—Movements that follow the path of a straight line.

low-maintenance tool—Offensive and defensive tools that require the least amount of training and practice to maintain proficiency. Low maintenance tools generally do not require preliminary stretching.

low-line kick—One of the two different classifications of a kick. A kick that is directed to targets below the assailant's waist level. (See high-line kick.)

lock—See joint lock.

M

maneuver—To manipulate into a strategically desired position.

MAP—An acronym that stands for moderate, aggressive, passive. MAP provides the practitioner with three possible responses to various grabs, chokes, and holds that occur from a standing position. See aggressive response, moderate response, and passive response.

martial arts—The "arts of war."

masking—The process of concealing your true feelings from your opponent by manipulating and managing your body language.

mechanics—(See body mechanics.)

mental attributes—The various cognitive qualities that enhance your fighting skills.

mental component—One of the three vital components of the CFA system. The mental component includes the cerebral aspects of fighting including the killer instinct, strategic and tactical development, analysis and integration, philosophy, and cognitive development. See physical component and spiritual component.

mesomorph—One of the three somatotypes. A body type classified by a high degree of muscularity and strength. The mesomorph possesses the ideal physique for unarmed combat. See ectomorph and endomorph.

mobility—A combative attribute. The ability to move your body quickly and freely while balanced. See footwork.

moderate response—One of the three possible counters when assaulted by a grab, choke, or hold from a standing position. Moderate response requires you to counter your opponent with a control and restraint (submission hold). See aggressive response and passive response.

modern martial art—A pragmatic combat art that has evolved to meet the demands and characteristics of the present time.

mounted position—A dominant ground-fighting position where a fighter straddles his opponent.

muscular endurance—The muscles' ability to perform the same motion or task repeatedly for a prolonged period of time.

muscular flexibility—The muscles' ability to move through maximum natural ranges.

muscular strength—The maximum force that can be exerted by a particular muscle or muscle group against resistance.

muscular/skeletal conditioning—An element of physical fitness that entails muscular strength, endurance, and flexibility.

N

naked choke—A throat choke executed from the chest to back position. This secure choke is executed with two hands and it can be performed while standing, kneeling, and ground fighting with the opponent.

neck crush – A powerful pain compliance technique used when the adversary buries his head in your chest to avoid being razed.

neutralize—See incapacitate.

neutral zone—The distance outside the kicking range at which neither the practitioner nor the assailant can touch the other.

nonaggressive physiology—Strategic body language used prior to initiating a first strike.

nontelegraphic movement—Body mechanics or movements that do not inform an assailant of your intentions.

nuclear ground-fighting tools—Specific grappling range tools designed to inflict immediate and irreversible damage. Nuclear tools and tactics include biting tactics, tearing tactics, crushing tactics, continuous choking tactics, gouging techniques, raking tactics, and all striking techniques.

O

offense—The armed and unarmed means and methods of attacking a criminal assailant.

offensive flow—Continuous offensive movements (kicks, blows, and strikes) with unbroken continuity that ultimately neutralize or terminate the opponent. See compound attack.

offensive reaction time—The elapsed time between target selection and target impaction.

one-mindedness—A state of deep concentration wherein you are free from all distractions (internal and external).

ostrich defense—One of the biggest mistakes one can make when defending against an opponent. This is when the practitioner looks away from that which he fears (punches, kicks, and strikes). His mentality is, "If I can't see it, it can't hurt me."

P

pain tolerance—Your ability to physically and psychologically withstand pain.

panic—The second stage of fear; overpowering fear. See fright and terror.

parry—A defensive technique: a quick, forceful slap that redirects an assailant's linear attack. There are two types of parries: horizontal and vertical.

passive response—One of the three possible counters when assaulted by a grab, choke, or hold from a standing position. Passive response requires you to nullify the assault without injuring your adversary. See aggressive response and moderate response.

patience—A combative attribute. The ability to endure and tolerate difficulty.

perception—Interpretation of vital information acquired from your senses when faced with a potentially threatening situation.

philosophical resolution—The act of analyzing and answering various questions concerning the use of violence in defense of yourself and others.

philosophy—One of the five aspects of CFA's mental component. A deep state of introspection whereby you methodically resolve critical questions concerning the use of force in defense of yourself or others.

physical attributes—The numerous physical qualities that enhance your combative skills and abilities.

physical component—One of the three vital components of the CFA system. The physical component includes the physical aspects of fighting, such as physical fitness, weapon/technique mastery, and combative attributes. See mental component and spiritual component.

physical conditioning—See combative fitness.

physical fitness—See combative fitness.

positional asphyxia—The arrangement, placement, or positioning of your opponent's body in such a way as to interrupt your breathing and cause unconsciousness or possibly death.

positioning—The spatial relationship of the assailant to the assailed person in terms of target exposure, escape, angle of attack, and various other strategic considerations.

postal attack - see going postal.

power—A physical attribute of armed and unarmed combat. The amount of force you can generate when striking an anatomical target.

power generators—Specific points on your body that generate impact power. There are three anatomical power generators: shoulders, hips, and feet.

precision—See accuracy.

preemptive strike—See first strike.

premise—An axiom, concept, rule, or any other valid reason to modify or go beyond that which has been established.

preparedness—A state of being ready for combat. There are three components of preparedness: affective preparedness, cognitive preparedness, and psychomotor preparedness.

probable reaction dynamics - The opponent's anticipated or predicted movements or actions during both armed and unarmed combat.

proficiency training—A CFA training methodology requiring the practitioner to execute a specific body weapon, technique, maneuver, or tactic over and over for a prescribed number of repetitions. See conditioning training and street training.

progressive indirect attack (PIA) – One of the five methods of attack. A progressive method of attack whereby the initial tool or technique is designed to set the opponent up for follow-up blows.

proxemics—The study of the nature and effect of man's personal space.

proximity—The ability to maintain a strategically safe distance from a threatening individual.

pseudospeciation—A combative attribute. The tendency to assign subhuman and inferior qualities to a threatening assailant.

psychological conditioning—The process of conditioning the mind for the horrors and rigors of real combat.

psychomotor preparedness—One of the three components of preparedness. Psychomotor preparedness means possessing all of the physical skills and attributes necessary to defeat a formidable adversary. See affective preparedness and cognitive preparedness.

punch—A quick, forceful strike of the fists.

punching range—One of the three ranges of unarmed combat. Punching range is the mid range of unarmed combat from which the fighter uses his hands to strike his assailant. See kicking range and grappling range.

punching-range tools—The various body weapons that are employed in the punching range of unarmed combat, including finger jabs, palm-heel strikes, rear cross, knife-hand strikes, horizontal and shovel hooks, uppercuts, and hammer-fist strikes. See grappling-range tools and kicking-range tools.

Q

qualities of combat—See attributes of combat.

quarter beat - One of the four beat classifications of the Widow Maker Program. Quarter beat strikes never break contact with the assailant's face. Quarter beat strikes are primarily responsible for creating the psychological panic and trauma when Razing.

R

range—The spatial relationship between a fighter and a threatening assailant.

range deficiency—The inability to effectively fight and defend in all ranges of combat (armed and unarmed).

range manipulation—A combative attribute. The strategic manipulation of combat ranges.

range proficiency—A combative attribute. The ability to effectively fight and defend in all ranges of combat (armed and unarmed).

ranges of engagement—See combat ranges.

ranges of unarmed combat—The three distances (kicking range, punching range, and grappling range) a fighter might physically engage with an assailant while involved in unarmed combat.

raze – To level, demolish or obliterate.

razer – One who performs the Razing methodology.

razing – The second phase of the Widow Maker Program. A series of vicious close quarter techniques designed to physically and psychologically extirpate a criminal attacker.

razing amplifier - a technique, tactic or procedure that magnifies the destructiveness of your razing technique.

reaction dynamics—see probable reaction dynamics.

reaction time—The elapsed time between a stimulus and the response to that particular stimulus. See offensive reaction time and defensive reaction time.

rear cross—A straight punch delivered from the rear hand that crosses from right to left (if in a left stance) or left to right (if in a right stance).

rear side—The side of the body furthest from the assailant. See lead side.

reasonable force—That degree of force which is not excessive for a particular event and which is appropriate in protecting yourself or others.

refinement—The strategic and methodical process of improving or perfecting.

relocation principle—Also known as relocating, this is a street-fighting tactic that requires you to immediately move to a new location (usually by flanking your adversary) after delivering a compound attack.

repetition—Performing a single movement, exercise, strike, or action continuously for a specific period.

research—A scientific investigation or inquiry.

rhythm—Movements characterized by the natural ebb and flow of related elements.

ritual-oriented training—Formalized training that is conducted without intrinsic purpose. See combat-oriented training and sport-oriented training.

S

safety—One of the three criteria for a CFA body weapon, technique, maneuver, or tactic. It means that the tool, technique, maneuver or tactic provides the least amount of danger and risk for the practitioner. See efficiency and effectiveness.

scissors hold—See guard position.

scorching – Quickly and inconspicuously applying oleoresin capsicum (hot pepper extract) on your fingertips and then razing your adversary.

self-awareness—One of the three categories of CFA awareness. Knowing and understanding yourself. This includes aspects of yourself which may provoke criminal violence and which will promote a proper and strong reaction to an attack. See criminal awareness and situational awareness.

self-confidence—Having trust and faith in yourself.

self-enlightenment—The state of knowing your capabilities, limitations, character traits, feelings, general attributes, and motivations. See self-awareness.

set—A term used to describe a grouping of repetitions.

shadow fighting—A CFA training exercise used to develop and refine your tools, techniques, and attributes of armed and unarmed combat.

sharking – A counter attack technique that is used when your adversary grabs your razing hand.

shielding wedge - a defensive maneuver used to counter an unarmed postal attack.

simple direct attack (SDA) – One of the five methods of attack. A method of attack whereby the practitioner delivers a solitary offense tool or technique. It may involve a series of discrete probes or one swift, powerful strike aimed at terminating the encounter.

situational awareness—One of the three categories of CFA awareness. A state of being totally alert to your immediate surroundings, including people, places, objects, and actions. (See criminal awareness and self-awareness.)

skeletal alignment—The proper alignment or arrangement of your body. Skeletal alignment maximizes the structural integrity of striking tools.

skills—One of the three factors that determine who will win a street fight. Skills refers to psychomotor proficiency with the tools and techniques of combat. See Attitude and Knowledge.

slipping—A defensive maneuver that permits you to avoid an assailant's linear blow without stepping out of range. Slipping can be accomplished by quickly snapping the head and upper torso sideways (right or left) to avoid the blow.

snap back—A defensive maneuver that permits you to avoid an assailant's linear and circular blows without stepping out of range. The snap back can be accomplished by quickly snapping the head backward to avoid the assailant's blow.

somatotypes—A method of classifying human body types or builds into three different categories: endomorph, mesomorph, and ectomorph. See endomorph, mesomorph, and ectomorph.

sparring—A training exercise where two or more fighters fight each other while wearing protective equipment.

speed—A physical attribute of armed and unarmed combat. The rate or a measure of the rapid rate of motion.

spiritual component—One of the three vital components of the CFA system. The spiritual component includes the metaphysical issues and aspects of existence. See physical component and mental component.

sport-oriented training—Training that is geared for competition and governed by a set of rules. See combat-oriented training and ritual-oriented training.

sprawling—A grappling technique used to counter a double- or single-leg takedown.

square off—To be face-to-face with a hostile or threatening assailant who is about to attack you.

stance—One of the many strategic postures you assume prior to or during armed or unarmed combat.

stick fighting—Fighting that takes place with either one or two sticks.

strategic positioning—Tactically positioning yourself to either escape, move behind a barrier, or use a makeshift weapon.

strategic/tactical development—One of the five elements of CFA's mental component.

strategy—A carefully planned method of achieving your goal of engaging an assailant under advantageous conditions.

street fight—A spontaneous and violent confrontation between two or more individuals wherein no rules apply.

street fighter—An unorthodox combatant who has no formal training. His combative skills and tactics are usually developed in the street by the process of trial and error.

street training—A CFA training methodology requiring the practitioner to deliver explosive compound attacks for 10 to 20 seconds. See condition ng training and proficiency training.

strength training—The process of developing muscular strength through systematic application of progressive resistance.

striking art—A combat art that relies predominantly on striking techniques to neutralize or terminate a criminal attacker.

striking shield—A rectangular shield constructed of foam and vinyl used to develop power in your kicks, punches, and strikes.

striking tool—A natural body weapon that impacts with the assailant's anatomical target.

strong side—The strongest and most coordinated side of your body.

structure—A definite and organized pattern.

style—The distinct manner in which a fighter executes or performs his combat skills.

stylistic integration—The purposeful and scientific collection of tools and techniques from various disciplines, which are strategically integrated and dramatically altered to meet three essential criteria: efficiency, effectiveness, and combative safety.

submission holds—Also known as control and restraint techniques, many of these locks and holds create sufficient pain to cause the adversary to submit.

system—The unification of principles, philosophies, rules, strategies, methodologies, tools, and techniques of a particular method of combat.

T

tactic—The skill of using the available means to achieve an end.

target awareness—A combative attribute that encompasses five strategic principles: target orientation, target recognition, target selection, target impaction, and target exploitation.

target exploitation—A combative attribute. The strategic maximization of your assailant's reaction dynamics during a fight. Target exploitation can be applied in both armed and unarmed encounters.

target impaction—The successful striking of the appropriate anatomical target.

target orientation—A combative attribute. Having a workable knowledge of the assailant's anatomical targets.

target recognition—The ability to immediately recognize appropriate anatomical targets during an emergency self-defense situation.

target selection—The process of mentally selecting the appropriate anatomical target for your self-defense situation. This is predicated on certain factors, including proper force response, assailant's positioning, and range.

target stare—A form of telegraphing in which you stare at the anatomical target you intend to strike.

target zones—The three areas in which an assailant's anatomical targets are located. (See zone one, zone two and zone three.)

technique—A systematic procedure by which a task is accomplished.

telegraphic cognizance—A combative attribute. The ability to recognize both verbal and non-verbal signs of aggression or assault.

telegraphing—Unintentionally making your intentions known to your adversary.

tempo—The speed or rate at which you speak.

terminate—To kill.

terror—The third stage of fear; defined as overpowering fear. See fright and panic.

timing—A physical and mental attribute of armed and unarmed combat. Your ability to execute a movement at the optimum moment.

tone—The overall quality or character of your voice.

tool—See body weapon.

traditional martial arts—Any martial art that fails to evolve and change to meet the demands and characteristics of its present environment.

traditional style/system—See traditional martial arts.

training drills—The various exercises and drills aimed at perfecting combat skills, attributes, and tactics.

trap and tuck – A counter move technique used when the adversary attempts to raze you during your quarter beat assault.

U

unified mind—A mind free and clear of distractions and focused on the combative situation.

use of force response—A combative attribute. Selecting the appropriate level of force for a particular emergency self-defense situation.

V

viciousness—A combative attribute. The propensity to be extremely violent and destructive often characterized by intense savagery.

violence—The intentional utilization of physical force to coerce, injure, cripple, or kill.

visualization—Also known as mental visualization or mental imagery. The purposeful formation of mental images and scenarios in the mind's eye.

W

warm-up—A series of mild exercises, stretches, and movements designed to prepare you for more intense exercise.

weak side—The weaker and more uncoordinated side of your body.

weapon and technique mastery—A component of CFA's physical component. The kinesthetic and psychomotor development of a weapon or combative technique.

weapon capability—An assailant's ability to use and attack with a particular weapon.

webbing - The first phase of the Widow Maker Program. Webbing is a two hand strike delivered to the assailant's chin. It is called Webbing because your hands resemble a large web that wraps around the enemy's face.

widow maker – One who makes widows by destroying husbands.

widow maker program – A CFA combat program specifically designed to teach the law abiding citizen how to use extreme force when faced with immediate threat of unlawful deadly criminal attack. The Widow Maker program is divided into two phases or methodologies: Webbing and Razing.

Y

yell—A loud and aggressive scream or shout used for various strategic reasons.

Z

zero beat – One of the four beat classifications of the Widow Maker, Feral Fighting and Savage Street Fighting Programs. Zero beat strikes are full pressure techniques applied to a specific target until it completely ruptures. They include gouging, crushing, biting, and choking techniques.

zone one—Anatomical targets related to your senses, including the eyes, temple, nose, chin, and back of neck.

zone three—Anatomical targets related to your mobility, including thighs, knees, shins, and instep.

zone two—Anatomical targets related to your breathing, including front of neck, solar plexus, ribs, and groin.

About Sammy Franco

With over 30 years of experience, Sammy Franco is one of the world's foremost authorities on armed and unarmed self-defense. Highly regarded as a leading innovator in combat sciences, Mr. Franco was one of the premier pioneers in the field of "reality-based" self-defense and martial arts instruction.

Sammy Franco is perhaps best known as the founder and creator of Contemporary Fighting Arts (CFA), a state-of-the-art offensive-based combat system that is specifically designed for real-world self-defense. CFA is a sophisticated and practical system of self-defense, designed specifically to provide efficient and effective methods to avoid, defuse, confront, and neutralize both armed and unarmed attackers.

Sammy Franco has frequently been featured in martial art magazines, newspapers, and appeared on numerous radio and television programs. Mr. Franco has also authored numerous books, magazine articles, and editorials, and has developed a popular library of instructional videos.

Sammy Franco's experience and credibility in the combat sciences is unequaled. One of his many accomplishments in this field includes the fact that he has earned the ranking of a Law Enforcement Master Instructor, and has designed, implemented, and taught officer survival training to the United States Border Patrol (USBP). He has instructed members of the US Secret Service, Military Special Forces,

Washington DC Police Department, Montgomery County, Maryland Deputy Sheriffs, and the US Library of Congress Police. Sammy Franco is also a member of the prestigious International Law Enforcement Educators and Trainers Association (ILEETA) as well as the American Society of Law Enforcement Trainers (ASLET) and he is listed in the "Who's Who Director of Law Enforcement Instructors."

Sammy Franco is a nationally certified Law Enforcement Instructor in the following curricula: PR-24 Side-Handle Baton, Police Arrest and Control Procedures, Police Personal Weapons Tactics, Police Power Handcuffing Methods, Police Oleoresin Capsicum Aerosol Training (OCAT), Police Weapon Retention and Disarming Methods, Police Edged Weapon Countermeasures and "Use of Force" Assessment and Response Methods.

Mr. Franco holds a Bachelor of Arts degree in Criminal Justice from the University of Maryland. He is a regularly featured speaker at a number of professional conferences and conducts dynamic and enlightening seminars on numerous aspects of self-defense and combat training.

On a personal level, Sammy Franco is an animal lover, who will go to great lengths to assist and rescue animals. Throughout the years, he's rescued everything from turkey vultures to goats. However, his most treasured moments are always spent with his beloved German Shepherd dogs.

For more information about Mr. Franco and his unique Contemporary Fighting Arts system, you can visit his website at: **SammyFranco.com** or follow him on twitter **@RealSammyFranco**

Other Books by Sammy Franco

THE WIDOW MAKER PROGRAM
Extreme Self-Defense for Deadly Force Situations
by Sammy Franco

The Widow Maker Program is a shocking and revolutionary fighting style designed to unleash extreme force when faced with the immediate threat of an unlawful deadly criminal attack. In this unique book, self-defense innovator Sammy Franco teaches you his brutal and unorthodox combat style that is virtually indefensible and utterly devastating. With over 250 photographs and detailed step-by-step instructions, The Widow Maker Program teaches you Franco's surreptitious Webbing and Razing techniques. When combined, these two fighting methods create an unstoppable force capable of destroying the toughest adversary. 8.5 x 5.5, paperback, photos, illus, 218 pages.

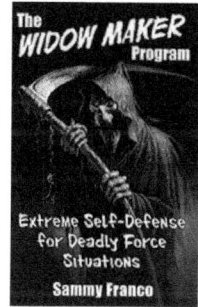

INVINCIBLE
Mental Toughness Techniques for Peak Performance
by Sammy Franco

Invincible is a treasure trove of battle-tested techniques and strategies for improving mental toughness in all aspects of life. It teaches you how to unlock the true power of your mind and achieve success in sports, fitness, high-risk professions, self-defense, and other peak performance activities. However, you don't have to be an athlete or warrior to benefit from this unique mental toughness book. In fact, the mental skills featured in this indispensable program can be used by anyone who wants to reach their full potential in life. 8.5 x 5.5, paperback, photos, illus, 250 pages.

MAXIMUM DAMAGE
Hidden Secrets Behind Brutal Fighting Combination
by Sammy Franco

Maximum Damage teaches you the quickest ways to beat your opponent in the street by exploiting his physical and psychological reactions in a fight. Learn how to stay two steps ahead of your adversary by knowing exactly how he will react to your strikes before they are delivered. In this unique book, reality based self-defense expert Sammy Franco reveals his unique Probable Reaction Dynamic (PRD) fighting method. Probable reaction dynamics are both a scientific and comprehensive offensive strategy based on the positional theory of

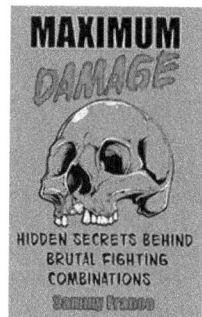

combat. Regardless of your style of fighting, PRD training will help you overpower your opponent by seamlessly integrating your strikes into brutal fighting combinations that are fast, ferocious and final! 8.5 x 5.5, paperback, 240 photos, illustrations, 238 pages.

SAVAGE STREET FIGHTING
Tactical Savagery as a Last Resort
by Sammy Franco

In this revolutionary book, Sammy Franco reveals the science behind his most primal street fighting method. Savage Street Fighting is a brutal self-defense system specifically designed to teach the law-abiding citizen how to use "Tactical Savagery" when faced with the immediate threat of an unlawful deadly criminal attack. Savage Street Fighting is systematically engineered to protect you when there are no other self-defense options left! With over 300 photographs and detailed step-by-step instructions, Savage Street Fighting is a must-have book for anyone concerned about real world self-defense. Now is the time to learn how to unleash your inner beast! 8.5 x 5.5, paperback, 317 photos, illustrations, 232 pages.

FIRST STRIKE
End a Fight in Ten Seconds or Less!
by Sammy Franco

Learn how to stop any attack before it starts by mastering the art of the preemptive strike. First Strike gives you an easy-to-learn yet highly effective self-defense game plan for handling violent close-quarter combat encounters. First Strike will teach you instinctive, practical and realistic self-defense techniques that will drop any criminal attacker to the floor with one punishing blow. By reading this book and by practicing, you will learn the hard-hitting skills necessary to execute a punishing first strike and ultimately prevail in a self-defense situation. And that's what it is all about: winning in as little time as possible. 8.5 x 5.5, paperback, photos, illustrations, 202 pages.

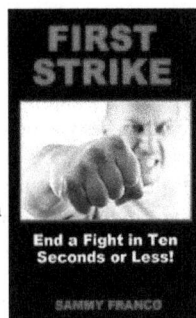

WAR MACHINE
How to Transform Yourself Into A Vicious & Deadly Street Fighter
by Sammy Franco

War Machine is a book that will change you for the rest of your life! When followed accordingly, War Machine will forge your mind, body and spirit into iron. Once armed with the mental and physical attributes of the War Machine, you will become a strong and confident warrior that can handle just about anything that life may throw your way. In essence, War

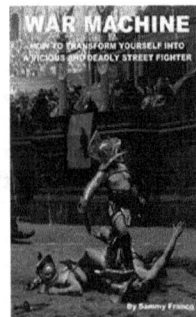

Machine is a way of life. Powerful, intense, and hard. 11 x 8.5, paperback, photos, illustrations, 210 pages.

KUBOTAN POWER
Quick and Simple Steps to Mastering the Kubotan Keychain
by Sammy Franco

With over 290 photographs and step-by-step instructions, Kubotan Power is the authoritative resource for mastering this devastating self-defense weapon. In this one-of-a-kind book, world-renowned self-defense expert, Sammy Franco takes thirty years of real-world teaching experience and gives you quick, easy and practical kubotan techniques that can be used by civilians, law enforcement personnel, or military professionals. The Kubotan is an incredible self-defense weapon that has helped thousands of people effectively defend themselves. Men, women, law enforcement officers, military, and security professionals alike, appreciate this small and discreet self-defense tool. Unfortunately, however, very little has been written about the kubotan, leaving it shrouded in both mystery and ignorance. As a result, most people don't know how to unleash the full power of this unique personal defense weapon. 8.5 x 5.5, paperback, 290 photos, illustrations, 204 pages.

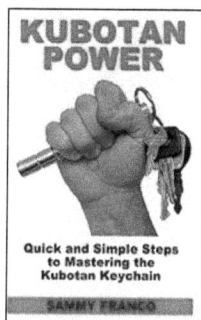

THE COMPLETE BODY OPPONENT BAG BOOK
by Sammy Franco

In this one-of-a-kind book, Sammy Franco teaches you the many hidden training features of the body opponent bag that will improve your fighting skills and boost your conditioning. With detailed photographs, step-by-step instructions, and dozens of unique workout routines, The Complete Body Opponent Bag Book is the authoritative resource for mastering this lifelike punching bag. The Complete Body Opponent Bag Book covers stances, punching, kicking, grappling techniques, mobility and footwork, targets, fighting ranges, training gear, time based workouts, punching and kicking combinations, weapons training, grappling drills, ground fighting, and dozens of workouts that will challenge you for years to come. 8.5 x 5.5, paperback, 139 photos, illustrations, 206 pages.

CONTEMPORARY FIGHTING ARTS, LLC
"Real World Self-Defense Since 1989"
www.SammyFranco.com